OECD Economic Surveys:
Australia
2017

BETTER POLICIES FOR BETTER LIVES

This document and any map included herein are without prejudice to the status of or sovereignty over any territory, to the delimitation of international frontiers and boundaries and to the name of any territory, city or area.

Please cite this publication as:
OECD (2017), OECD Economic Surveys: Australia 2017, OECD Publishing, Paris.
http://dx.doi.org/10.1787/eco_surveys-aus-2017-en

ISBN 978-92-64-27149-4 (print)
ISBN 978-92-64-27150-0 (PDF)
ISBN 978-92-64-27151-7 (epub)

Series: OECD Economic Surveys
ISSN 0376-6438 (print)
ISSN 1609-7513 (online)

OECD Economic Surveys: Australia
ISSN 1995-3089 (print)
ISSN 1999-0146 (online)

The statistical data for Israel are supplied by and under the responsibility of the relevant Israeli authorities. The use of such data by the OECD is without prejudice to the status of the Golan Heights, East Jerusalem and Israeli settlements in the West Bank under the terms of international law.

Photo credits: Cover © skyearth/Shutterstock.com.

Corrigenda to OECD publications may be found on line at: www.oecd.org/about/publishing/corrigenda.htm.

© OECD 2017

Table of contents

Thematic chapters

Boxes

Tables

This Survey is published on the responsibility of the Economic and Development Review Committee (EDRC) of the OECD, which is charged with the examination of the economic situation of member countries.

The economic situation and policies of Australia were reviewed by the Committee on the 12th of December, 2016. The draft report was then revised in the light of the discussions and given final approval as the agreed report of the whole Committee on the 3rd of January, 2017.

The Secretariat's draft report was prepared for the Committee by Philip Hemmings and Vassiliki Koutsogeorgopoulou under the supervision of Piritta Sorsa. Statistical research analysis was provided by Taejin Park. Administrative assistance was provided by Anthony Bolton and Brigitte Beyeler.

The previous Survey of Australia was issued in December 2014.

Follow OECD Publications on:

 http://twitter.com/OECD_Pubs

 http://www.facebook.com/OECDPublications

 http://www.linkedin.com/groups/OECD-Publications-4645871

 http://www.youtube.com/oecdilibrary

 http://www.oecd.org/oecddirect/

This book has...   StatLinks ⫸ᵢₗ s▯

A service that delivers Excel® files from the printed page!

Look for the *StatLinks* ᵢₗs▯ at the bottom of the tables or graphs in this book. To download the matching Excel® spreadsheet, just type the link into your Internet browser, starting with the *http://dx.doi.org* prefix, or click on the link from the e-book edition.

Basic statistics of Australia

(Numbers in parentheses refer to the OECD average)*

LAND, PEOPLE AND ELECTORAL CYCLE

Population (million)	23.9		Population density per km^2	3.1	(35.1)
Under 15 (%)	18.9	(18.0)	Life expectancy (years, 2014)	82.4	(80.9)
Over 65 (%)	14.9	(16.3)	Men (2013)	80.1	(77.8)
Foreign-born (%, 2014)	28.1		Women (2013)	84.3	(83.1)
Latest 5-year average growth (%)	1.4	(0.4)	Latest general election		July 2016

ECONOMY

Gross domestic product (GDP)			Value added shares (%, 2014)		
In current prices (billion USD)	1 229.6		Primary sector	2.6	(2.4)
In current prices (billion AUD)	1 633.8		Industry including mining and construction	25.4	(26.6)
Latest 5-year average real growth (%)	2.7	(1.9)	Services	72.0	(70.9)
Per capita (000 USD PPP)	46.7	(4.1)			

GENERAL GOVERNMENT
Per cent of GDP

Expenditure[a]	35.7	(41.7)	Gross financial debt[a]	44.2	(111.6)
Revenue	34.2	(38.5)	Net financial debt[a]	-14.6	(72.7)

EXTERNAL ACCOUNTS

Exchange rate (AUD per USD)	1.329		Main exports (% of total merchandise exports)		
PPP exchange rate (USA = 1)	1.462		Crude materials, inedible, except fuels		31.8
In per cent of GDP			Mineral fuels, lubricants and related materials		25.3
Exports of goods and services	19.3	(5.5)	Food and live animals		14.3
Imports of goods and services	21.6	(5.1)	Main imports (% of total merchandise imports)		
Current account balance	-4.8	(0.2)	Machinery and transport equipment		39.6
Net international investment position	-56.8		Miscellaneous manufactured articles		15.1
			Manufactured goods		12.2

LABOUR MARKET, SKILLS AND INNOVATION

Employment rate for 15-64 year-olds (%)	72.2	(66.2)	Unemployment rate, Labour Force Survey (age 15 and over) (%)	6.1	(6.8)
Men	77.5	(74.1)	Youth (age 15-24, %)	13.1	(13.9)
Women	66.8	(58.5)	Long-term unemployed (1 year and over, %)	1.4	(2.2)
Participation rate for 15-64 year-olds (%)	76.9	(71.2)	Tertiary educational attainment 25-64 year-olds (%)	42.9	(35.7)
Average hours worked per year	1 665	(1 766)	Gross domestic expenditure on R&D (% of GDP, 2013)	2.1	(2.4)

ENVIRONMENT

Total primary energy supply per capita (toe)	5.5	(4.1)	CO_2 emissions from fuel combustion per capita (tonnes, 2014)	15.8	(9.4)
Renewables (% of total)	6.5	(9.6)	Water abstractions per capita (1 000 m^3, 2011)	0.6	
Fine particulate matter concentration (PM2.5, µg/m^3)	6.7	(14.5)	Municipal waste per capita (tonnes, 2011)	0.6	(0.5)

SOCIETY

Income inequality (Gini coefficient, 2014[b])	0.337	(0.31)	Education outcomes (PISA score)		
Relative poverty rate (%, 2014[b])	12.8	(11.0)	Reading	503	(496)
Median equivalised household income (000 USD PPP, 2014)	31.3	(22.4)	Mathematics	494	(494)
Public and private spending (% of GDP)			Science	510	(501)
Health care, current expenditure	9.3	(9.1)	Share of women in parliament (%, August 2016)	31.9	(27.8)
Pensions (2014[b])	6.9	(9.1)	Net official development assistance (% of GNI)	0.27	(0.39)
Education (primary, secondary, post sec. non tertiary, 2013)	3.9	(3.7)			

Better life index: *www.oecdbetterlifeindex.org*

a) 2014 for the OECD aggregate

b) 2013 for the OECD aggregate.

c) 2011 for the OECD aggregate.

* Data refer to 2015 unless otherwise stated. Where the OECD aggregate is not provided in the source database, a simple OECD average of latest available data is calculated where data exist for at least 29 member countries.

Source: Calculations based on data extracted from the databases of the following organisations: OECD, International Energy Agency, World Bank, International Monetary Fund and Inter-Parliamentary Union.

Acronyms

ACCC	Australian Competition and Consumer Commission
ACOLA	Australian Council of Learned Academies
AIMS	Australian Institute of Marine Science
ANTO	Australian Nuclear Science and Technology Organisation
APRA	Australian Prudential Regulation Authority
APS	Australian Public Service
ARC	Australian Research Council
ATO	Australian Taxation Office
CCS	Carbon Capture and Storage
CSIRO	Commonwealth Scientific and Industrial Research Organisation
CRC	Cooperative Research Centres
DSP	Disability Support Pension
DTA	Digital Transformation Agency
DTO	Digital Transformation Office
ERA	Excellence in Research for Australia
ESCCLP	Early Stage Venture Capital Limited Partnerships
GDP	Gross Domestic Product
GERD	Gross expenditure on R&D
GFC	Global-Financial Crisis
GHG	Greenhouse Gas
GST	Goods and Services Tax
HSSA	Health Services Satellite Account
ICT	Information and communications technology
IP	Intellectual Property
ISA	Innovation and Science Australia
KBC	Knowledge-Based Capital
LNG	Liquefied Natural Gas
LVR	Loan-To-Valuation
MNO	Mobile-Network Operator
MVNO	Mobile Virtual Network Operator
MRFF	Medical Research Future Fund
NBN	National Broadband Network
NCC	National Competition Council
NDIS	National Disability Insurance Scheme
NHMRC	National Health and Medical Research Council
NICTA	National ICT Australia Ltd
NISA	National Innovation and Science Agenda
PGPA	Public Governance and Accountability Act
PSRA	Public Sector Research Agency

R&D	Research and Development
RBA	Reserve Bank of Australia
RBG	Research Block Grants
RTP	Research Training Programme
RSP	Research Support Programme
SIM	Subscriber Identity Module
SME	Small and Medium Enterprise
STEM	Science, Technology, Engineering and Mathematics
TBL	Triple Bottom Line
TFP	Total-Factor Productivity
TTO	Technology Transfer Office
VAT	Value Added Tax
VHA	Vodaphone-Hutchison Australia

Executive summary

- *Supporting rebalancing with macroeconomic policies*
- *Sustaining growth by bolstering the environment for business innovation*
- *Addressing inequality and ensuring economic rebalancing delivers more inclusive growth*

Supporting rebalancing with macroeconomic policies

Commodity prices and GDP growth

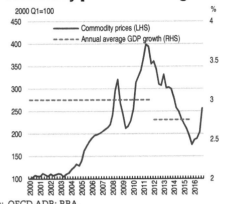

Source: OECD ADB; RBA.

StatLink ⟨⟩ http://dx.doi.org/10.1787/888933456594

Australia's economy has enjoyed considerable success in recent decades, reflecting strong macroeconomic policy, structural reform and the long commodity boom. Living standards and well-being are generally high, though challenges remain in gender gaps and in greenhouse-gas emissions, and further challenges arise from population ageing. The economy is now rebalancing following the end of the commodity boom, supported by macroeconomic policies and currency depreciation. The strengthening non-mining sector is projected to support output growth of around 3% in 2018 and spur further reduction in the unemployment rate. Low interest rates have supported aggregate demand but are also ramping up risk-taking by investors and driving house prices and mortgage lending to historical highs.

Sustaining growth by bolstering the environment for business innovation

R&D spending as a share of GDP

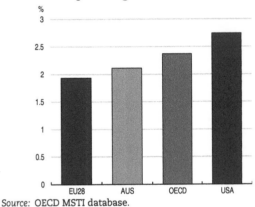

Source: OECD MSTI database.

StatLink ⟨⟩ http://dx.doi.org/10.1787/888933456603

Improving competition and other framework conditions that influence the absorption and development of innovation are key for restoring productivity growth. Innovation requires labour and capital markets that facilitate new business models. Productivity growth could be boosted through stronger collaboration between business and research sectors in R&D activity. The government's reform programme, notably the *National Innovation and Science Agenda*, is providing welcome impetus to reform.

Addressing inequality and ensuring economic rebalancing delivers more inclusive growth

Real increase of household income and wealth, 2004-14

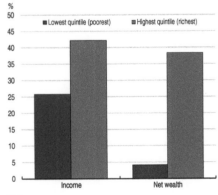

Source: ABS.

StatLink ⟨⟩ http://dx.doi.org/10.1787/888933456618

Australia's adjustment to the end of the commodity boom has not been painless. Unemployment has risen, and there are increasing concerns about inequality. In addition, large socioeconomic gaps between Australia's indigenous community and the rest of the population remain. Developing innovation-related skills will be important for the underprivileged and those displaced by economic restructuring, and can help reduce gender wage gaps.

MAIN FINDINGS	KEY RECOMMENDATIONS
Macroeconomic and financial-market regulation policies	
Low interest rates have fuelled high house prices and generated substantial mortgage borrowing	Maintain tight macro-prudential measures Facilitate housing supply increases through improved planning regulation
There is fiscal space available to support the economy if required	Use all policy levers to support the economy if downside risks materialise, relying more heavily on fiscal policy.
Banking remains highly concentrated, potentially compromising competition and making Australia vulnerable to "too big to fail" risks	Reduce banks' implicit guarantees by developing a loss absorbing and recapitalisation framework
Fiscal reform	
Global commodity swings can have large budgetary effects	Consider a spending ceiling to contain expenditure growth in booms and targeting debt in the long term Create stabilisation funds using resource revenues, or make greater use of existing funds, to insulate the budget from commodity price changes
Change the tax mix to better support growth	Further shift from corporate income taxes and inefficient taxes, raise the Goods and Services Tax and land taxes Make the R&D Tax Incentive more effective, for instance by combining an eligibility threshold with an increase in the expenditure cap
Maintaining quality public services given low growth in public expenditure is a challenge	Encourage more innovation in public services by opening up procurement to more bidders and further development of digital government services Reduce the number of support schemes for innovative SMEs
Boosting productivity through a more innovation-friendly business environment	
Business framework conditions could better support the absorption and creation of innovation through stronger competition and resource allocation	Improve competition law, notably by strengthening the definition of abuse of dominant position Adjust insolvency legislation Increase labour mobility, for instance by lower interstate differences in education and training programmes Encourage market entry by innovative business. Use competition policy tools to combat resistance by incumbents and adjust sectoral regulation quickly as new firms and industries emerge Facilitate the entry of a fourth operator in mobile telephony via a spectrum auction
Research-business collaboration is weak and decision making in the innovation system fragmented	Put a greater weight, as envisaged, on collaboration in university funding and develop a more coordinated approach to industry placements for research students to strengthen the linkages between research and business sectors Implement the common approach across public-sector research organisations for assessing research outcomes and impacts Develop a more integrated, "whole-of-government" approach to science, research and innovation and consolidate innovation support programmes
Helping output growth and inclusiveness, deepening skills	
Inclusiveness is being eroded	Avoid freezing welfare pay outs as part of fiscal restraint so as to not compromise inclusiveness Continue developing an investment approach to welfare policy that focuses on vulnerable groups where the returns to policy are greatest
Skills for innovation are weak	Widen the scope of subsidies for innovation-related subjects beyond STEM (e.g. innovation-related arts disciplines)
Environmental sustainability	
New greenhouse-gas reduction targets have been set	Strengthen the recently introduced safeguard mechanism should the Emissions Reduction Fund require additional support to achieve greenhouse-gas reduction

Assessment and recommendations

- *Macroeconomic developments and near-term prospects: post-boom adjustment continues*
- *Monetary and financial-market policy: coping with low interest rates*
- *Fiscal consolidation, tax and spending reform*
- *Encouraging business productivity and innovation through framework conditions*
- *Encouraging productivity and innovation through R&D policy*
- *Addressing inequality, enhancing inclusiveness and deepening skills*
- *Tackling environmental challenges: progress in greenhouse-gas emission policy*

The statistical data for Israel are supplied by and under the responsibility of the relevant Israeli authorities. The use of such data by the OECD is without prejudice to the status of the Golan Heights, East Jerusalem and Israeli settlements in the West Bank under the terms of international law.

Following an impressive 25 consecutive years of output growth, Australia's gross domestic product per capita is high and the country generally ranks favourably in well-being (Figure 1). Despite the end of the global commodity super-cycle, the economy continues to perform well. The rebalancing of economic activity from commodity investment to other activities is well advanced, facilitated by monetary and fiscal policies, currency depreciation, and flexible labour and product markets.

However, Australia's economy shares the global risk of a "low-growth trap". Along with many OECD countries, productivity growth has slowed since its peak in the 1990s (Figure 2) but remains in line with its longer term average. Despite encouraging recent productivity growth, population aging (the number of Australians over 65 years of age will more than double by 2055) means the country's growth prospects depend crucially on strong productivity growth which, in turn, requires greater capacity for absorbing and generating new innovations. This is the subject of this *Survey's* in-depth examination of innovation and related policies and the focus of a recent government initiative (the *National Innovation and Science Agenda*; Australian Government, 2015a).

Furthermore, inclusiveness has been eroded. The Gini coefficient has been drifting up and households in upper income brackets have benefited disproportionally from Australia's long period of economic growth. Real incomes for the top quintile of households grew by more than 40% between 2004 and 2014 while those for the lowest quintile only grew by about 25% (Figure 3). Strong growth has pulled the incomes of households with wage earners further ahead of households reliant on transfers or pensions, which dominate the lower end of the income distribution. Furthermore, recent economic development has been strongly skill biased – partly because scale effects have amplified returns to some already high-paid segments of the labour market – widening the wage distribution. This partly explains the increasing share of income going to the very top end of the income distribution. In addition, large socioeconomic gaps between Australia's indigenous population (Box 1) and the rest of the population remain and there is room to reduce gender imbalance (Figures 3 and 4).

Against this background the main messages of this *Survey* are:

- Strong macroeconomic and financial-sector institutions and policies have supported strong economic growth and high living standards.

- Merely maintaining long-run average productivity growth jeopardises this success; a renewed emphasis on structural reforms in particular those that help boost Australia's capacity to absorb and generate innovation is required.

- Widening income inequalities and longstanding issues of inclusion (notably Australia's indigenous population) call for an ongoing emphasis on policies to ensure equitable opportunities for engaging in the labour market through skills acquisition and active labour market policies, especially policies that address these concerns while also enhancing productivity.

Figure 1. **GDP per capita is high and well-being indicators compare favourably**

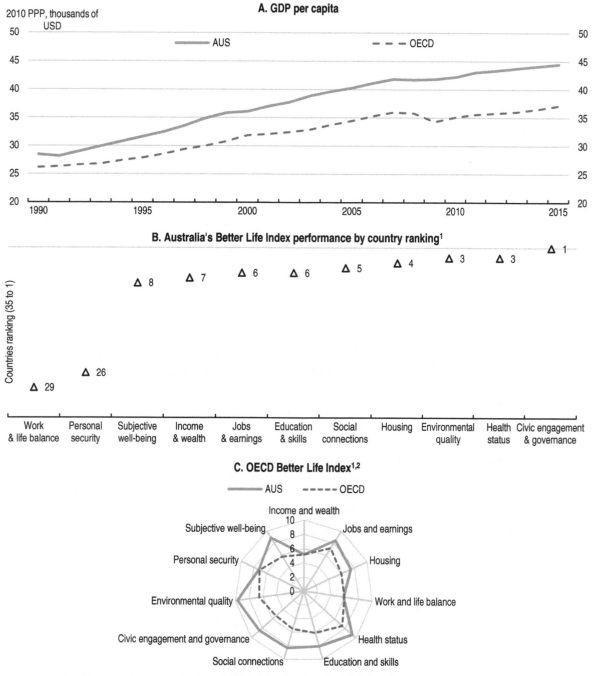

1. Each well-being dimension is measured using one to three indications from the OECD Better Life Indicator set with equal weights.
2. Indicators are normalised by re-scaling to be from 0 (worst) to 10 (best).
Source: OECD (2016), OECD National Accounts Statistics (database); OECD (2016), "Better Life Index 2016", OECD Social and Welfare Statistics (database).

StatLink 🔗 *http://dx.doi.org/10.1787/888933456622*

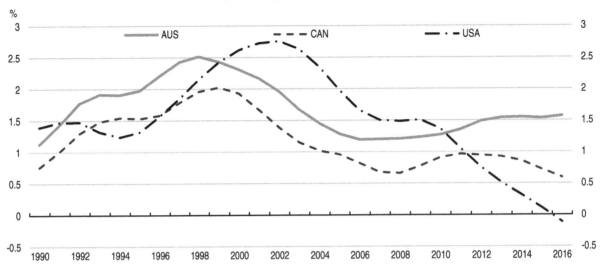

Figure 2. **Productivity growth has slowed**

Labour productivity growth (per hour worked)[1]

1. Data smoothed by the Hodrick-Prescott filter.
Source: The Conference Board (2016), The Conference Board Total Economy Database, May 2016.

StatLink ⟨⟨⟨ *http://dx.doi.org/10.1787/888933456634*

Box 1. Progress on closing the outcome gaps between the indigenous population and the rest of the population

Indigenous Australians account for around 3% of the total population, but around 45% of the population in rural and remote areas. Addressing indigenous disadvantage is a priority across all levels of government in Australia, with targets agreed and set by the Council of Australian Governments to improve outcomes. The policy function at the Federal level sits within the Prime Minister's department and the Prime Minister delivers an annual update to Parliament on the extent of progress made, in the Closing the Gap report. Progress is generally reported based on the extent to which the difference in outcomes for indigenous compared to non-indigenous Australians has been reduced.

The 2016 Closing the Gap report indicated:

● targets on track: halving the gap in child mortality by 2018; and halving the gap in Year 12 attainment by 2020

● targets not on track: closing the gap on life expectancy; halving the gap in employment by 2018; closing the gap between indigenous and non-indigenous school attendance; and halving the gap for indigenous children in reading, writing and numeracy (although four of the eight measures are on track)

● it is too early to gauge whether the target will be met for 95% of all indigenous four year olds to be enrolled in early childhood education by 2025.

The Productivity Commission's annual report on indigenous disadvantage (Productivity Commission, 2016) also highlights that progress towards better socio-economic outcomes remains mixed. The report also draws attention to the lack of rigorously evaluated programmes in the area of indigenous policy.

Figure 3. **Inequality has been rising**

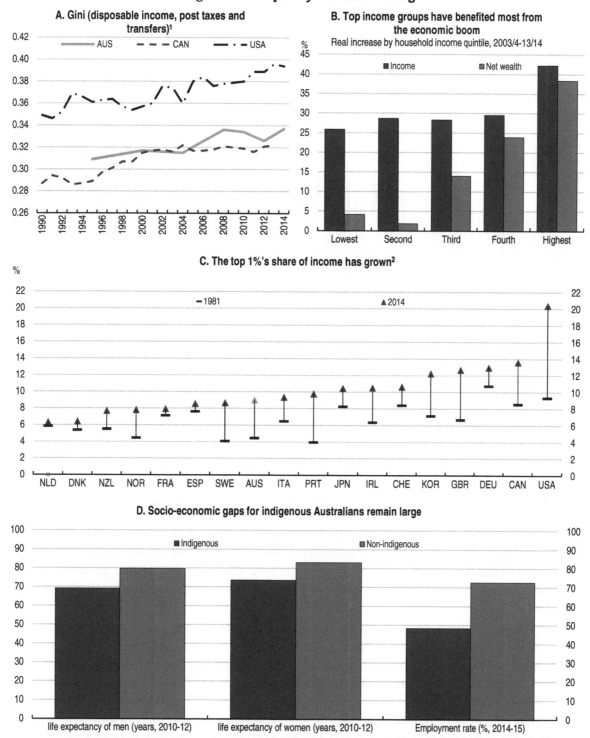

A. Gini (disposable income, post taxes and transfers)[1]

B. Top income groups have benefited most from the economic boom
Real increase by household income quintile, 2003/4-13/14

C. The top 1%'s share of income has grown[2]

D. Socio-economic gaps for indigenous Australians remain large

1. The Gini coefficient is based on the comparison of cumulative proportions of the population against cumulative proportions of income they receive, and it ranges between 0 in the case of perfect equality and 1 in the case of perfect inequality. New income definition applied for 2012 onwards (for United States, 2013 onwards).
2. Shares of top 1% incomes in total pre-tax income, 1980 – 2014 (or closest available period). For further details, *http://wid.world/*.
Source: OECD (2016), OECD Income Distribution database; ABS (2016), 6523.0 – Household Income and Wealth, Australia, 2013–14; WID.world (2016), The World Wealth and Income Database; Australian Department of the Prime Minister and Cabinet (2016), Closing the gap: Prime Minister's Report 2016; ABS (2016), 4714.0 – National Aboriginal and Torres Strait Islander Social Survey, Australia, 2014–15.

StatLink ᗑᔎᔗ *http://dx.doi.org/10.1787/888933456641*

Figure 4. **Australia's gender wage gap is larger than many**

Gender wage gap[1], 2014 or latest

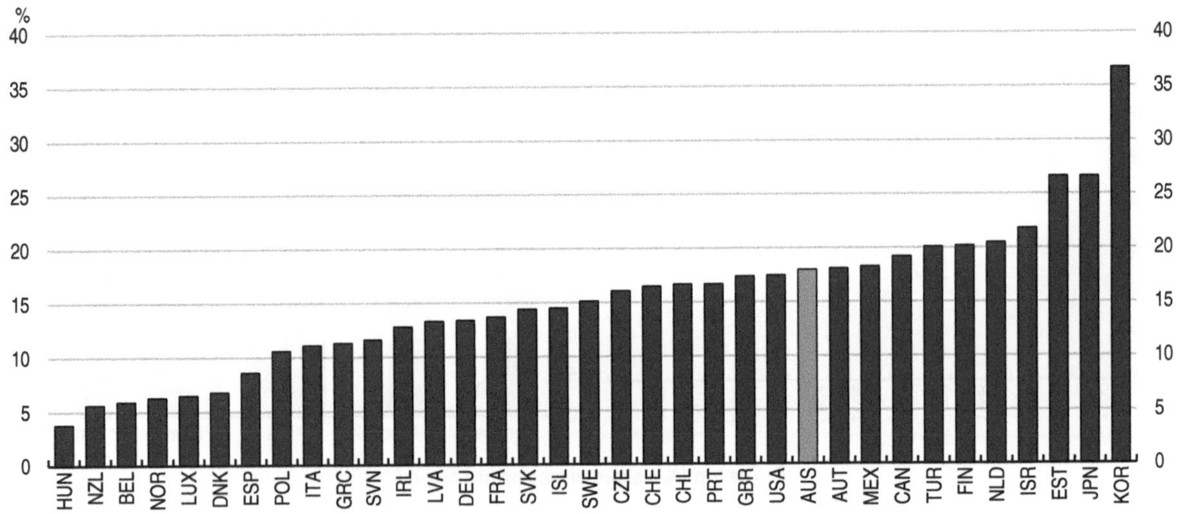

1. The gender wage gap is defined as the difference between male and female median wages divided by the male median wages.
Source: OECD (2016), OECD Gender Data Portal.

StatLink ᵐˢ⁴ http://dx.doi.org/10.1787/888933456650

Macroeconomic developments and near-term prospects: post-boom adjustment continues

Australia's output growth remained resilient during the global financial crisis thanks to a prompt macroeconomic policy response, high commodity prices and a resilient financial system (Figure 5). The significant economic adjustment to the commodity super cycle, which has dominated cyclical development over the past decade or so, has proceeded relatively smoothly (Figure 5). There have been large falls in resource-sector investment, from 9% of GDP towards 4.5%, and falls in resource-sector employment, partly because several large multi-year construction projects have reached, or are close to, completion. In addition, declines in global commodity prices from their peak in 2011, notably for iron ore and coal, have curtailed plans for new investment and prompted cost-cutting by producers, although commodity prices have increased in recent times. As in many other developed economies, Australia now faces the risk of low growth and lacklustre private-sector investment due to pessimistic expectations and weakening global trade.

Markets have been redeploying resources and reducing macroeconomic tensions reasonably effectively so far, helped by flexibility-oriented policy settings for labour and capital, and by supportive macroeconomic policy. Exchange-rate depreciation has proven a key channel, spurring non-resource-sector exports, such as inbound tourism (Figure 6). The reallocation of labour resources is echoed in state-level employment trends, with strong employment growth in New South Wales and Victoria countering low growth in the resource-rich states of Queensland and Western Australia. Net international migration has proved a shock absorber in Australia, as the influx of labour during the commodity boom has been reversing (Figure 6).

Consumer-price inflation and wage growth remain subdued. Consumer-price inflation has been below the Reserve Bank of Australia's (RBA's) medium-term target range of 2-3% for several quarters. Also, inflation expectations and nominal-wage growth have trended

Figure 5. **Output growth has weakened, unemployment is up, investment is down**

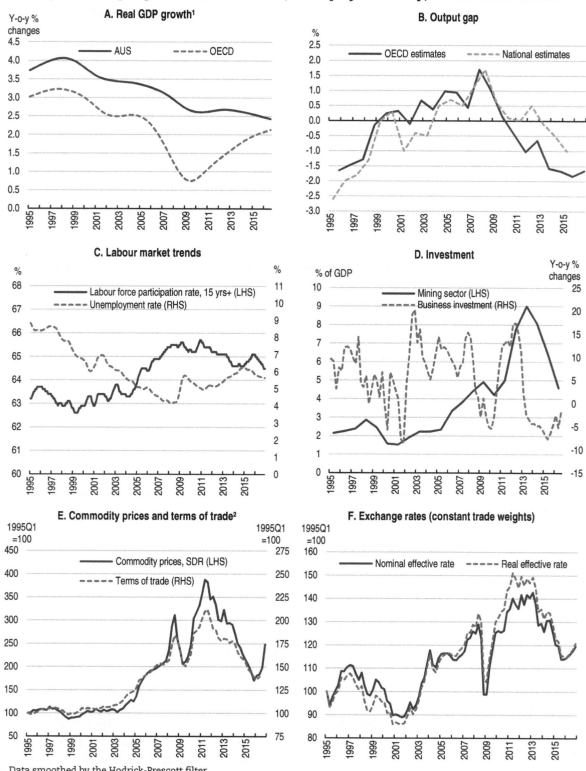

1. Data smoothed by the Hodrick-Prescott filter.
2. Terms of trade is the ratio of export and import prices.

Source: OECD (2016), OECD Analytical database; ABS (2016), 6202.0 – Labour Force, Australia; ABS (2016), 5204.0 – Australian System of National Accounts, 2014-15; ABS (2016), 5206.0 – Australian National Accounts: National Income, Expenditure and Product, Jun 2016; Reserve Bank of Australia; The Australian Treasury.

StatLink ᵐˢᵖ *http://dx.doi.org/10.1787/888933456664*

Figure 6. **Rebalancing is seen in services exports, employment and migration**

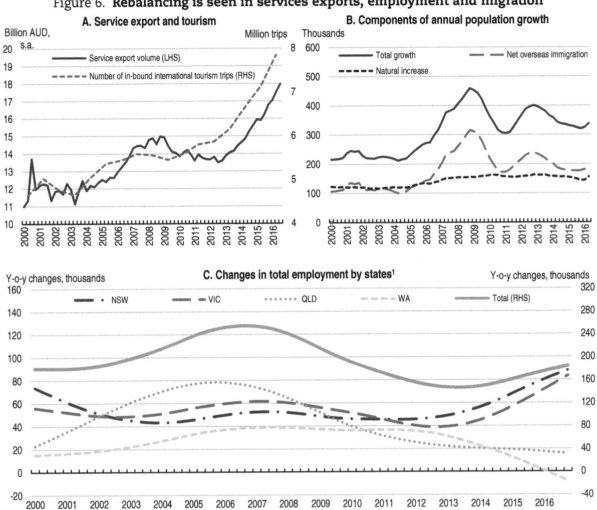

1. Data smoothed by the Hodrick-Prescott filter.
Source: ABS (2016), 5302.0 – Balance of Payments and International Investment Position; ABS (2016), 5249.0 – Australian National Accounts: Tourism Satellite Account; ABS (2016), 3101.0 – Australian Demographic Statistics; ABS (2016), 6291.0.55.003 – Labour Force, Australia, Detailed, Quarterly, Nov 2016.

StatLink http://dx.doi.org/10.1787/888933456671

down (Figure 7). Wage growth has been at record lows partly because of ongoing slack in the labour market, including in part-time employment where many employees wish to work longer hours. In addition, the share of part-time employment continues to rise.

Subdued nominal GDP growth has been weighing on revenues, making it harder to reach the government's fiscal goals (see below). Australia has a sizeable current account deficit though this is expected to narrow in the coming years. Economic risk from the persistent current account deficit is not considered large because a large proportion of foreign-held debt is either denominated in Australian dollars or is hedged against exchange-rate fluctuations (Figure 8). Australia's total debt burden has been steadily increasing, however it remains middle ranking in international comparison (Figure 9). Also, the Australian government only issues in Australian dollars. Household debt, while relatively high, is concentrated in high income households, and matched with rising asset values and low interest rates. Debt servicing to income ratios remain low (see discussion on macroprudential measures below).

Figure 7. **Consumer-price inflation and wage growth are slowing**

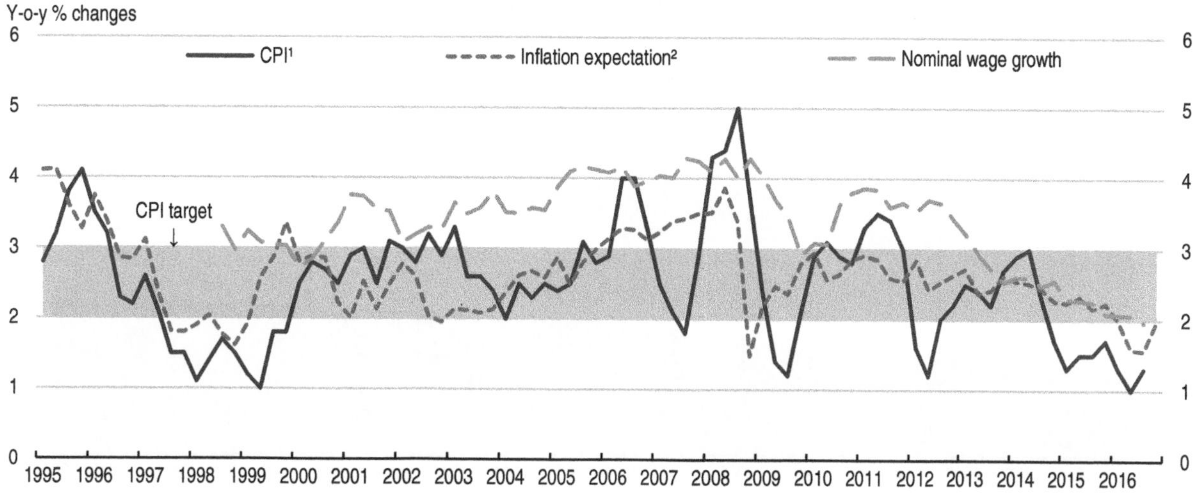

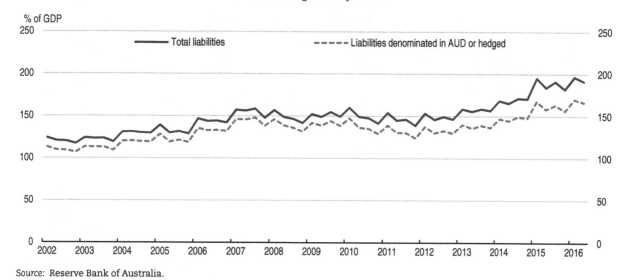

1. Excludes interest and tax changes.
2. Average annual inflation rate implied by the difference between 10-year nominal bond yield and 10-year inflation indexed bond yield.
Source: Reserve Bank of Australia (2016); ABS (2016), 6345.0 – Wage Price Index, Australia, Sep 2016.

StatLink *http://dx.doi.org/10.1787/888933456686*

Figure 8. **Australia's gross foreign liabilities continue to grow but remain largely denominated in AUD or are hedged**
Gross foreign liability stocks

Source: Reserve Bank of Australia.

StatLink *http://dx.doi.org/10.1787/888933456696*

Looking forward, OECD projections anticipate a slow pick-up in activity in the medium-term. The OECD Economic Outlook of autumn 2016 projected output growth for 2016 and 2017 of a little over 2½ %, rising to 3% for 2018 (Table 1). Since the projection was finalised, data releases showed that the economy shrank by 0.5% in Q3 of 2016. However, this outcome is expected to mean annual growth will only be slightly slower than in the projection given the largely temporary factors, including unseasonal factors behind the Q3 result. Sectoral shifts in investment will continue. The projections incorporate further shrinkage in mining investment, though at a slower pace, and a continued rise in

Figure 9. **Total debt has increased and household debt is above average**

A. Trends in debt by sector

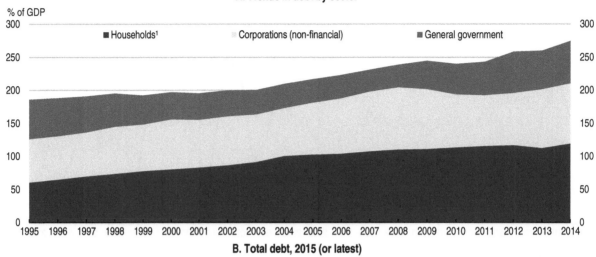

B. Total debt, 2015 (or latest)

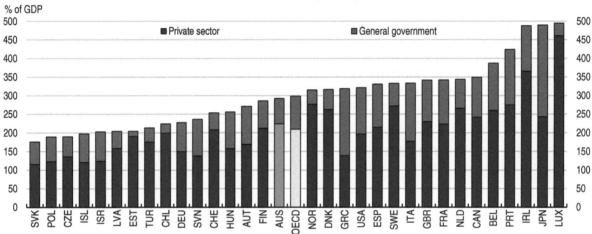

C. Household debt[1], 2015 (or latest)

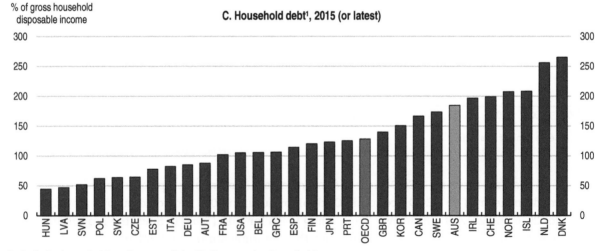

1. Includes households and non-profit institutions serving households.
Source: OECD (2017), OECD National Accounts (database).

StatLink ⫘⫘ *http://dx.doi.org/10.1787/888933456701*

non-commodity investment. Record low interest rates, currency depreciation and favourable business conditions on other fronts will support the investment. New liquefied-natural-gas (LNG) production following the completion of new facilities will continue to boost exports. Employment growth in non-mining activities will bring further declines in the rate of unemployment and support aggregate household income, and boost consumption. The pick-up in activity is not expected to generate significant inflationary pressure due to remaining economic slack.

Table 1. **Macroeconomic indicators and projections**

Annual percentage change, volume (2014 prices)

	2013			2016	2017	2018
	Current prices (billion AUD)	2014	2015	(projected)		
GDP	1,560	2.8	2.4	2.7	2.6	3.1
Private consumption	856	2.8	2.7	2.7	2.6	3.0
Government consumption	281	0.9	3.5	3.7	1.7	2.0
Gross fixed capital formation	431	-1.9	-3.1	-0.2	-0.9	1.5
Housing	73	6.9	10.0	7.7	6.0	3.5
Business	309	-4.8	-6.4	-4.7	-3.2	0.5
of which mining[1]	115	-8.5	-17.3	..	..	..
Government	50	3.5	-5.0	9.6	-2.4	2.5
Final domestic demand	1,568	1.2	1.3	2.2	1.6	2.5
Stockbuilding[2]	0	0.1	0.0	-0.9	0.0	0.0
Total domestic demand	1,568	1.2	1.3	1.3	1.6	2.4
Exports of goods and services	318	6.9	5.9	7.1	7.0	7.1
Imports of goods and services	326	-1.1	1.8	-0.2	1.9	3.8
Net exports[2]	-8	1.6	0.8	1.4	0.9	0.6
Other indicators (growth rates, unless specified)						
Potential GDP	..	2.8	2.6	2.5	2.4	2.3
Output gap[3]	..	-1.7	-1.8	-1.7	-1.5	-0.8
Employment	..	0.7	1.9	1.6	1.3	1.6
Unemployment rate	..	6.1	6.1	5.7	5.5	5.3
GDP deflator	..	0.2	-0.6	0.3	1.9	1.8
Consumer price index	..	2.5	1.5	1.3	1.8	2.1
Core consumer prices	..	2.4	2.1	1.6	1.7	2.1
Household saving ratio, net[4]	..	9.0	7.1	8.0	7.8	7.4
Trade balance[5]	..	0.1	-1.6	..	..	..
Current account balance[5]	..	-2.9	-4.8	-3.5	-2.5	-1.9
General government fiscal balance[5]	..	-2.3	-1.8	-2.6	-2.0	-1.5
Underlying government fiscal balance[3]	..	-1.5	-1.5	-1.8	-1.2	-1.1
Underlying government primary balance[3]	..	-0.8	-0.9	-1.3	-0.7	-0.5
General government gross debt[5]	..	42.1	44.3	45.4	45.1	44.6
General government net debt[5]	..	-13.1	-14.3	-11.4	-8.9	-6.9
Three-month money market rate, average	..	2.7	2.3	2.0	1.8	2.3
Ten-year government bond yield, average	..	3.7	2.7	2.2	2.0	2.3

1. Data are based on a financial year.
2. Contributions to changes in real GDP, actual amount in the first column.
3. As a percentage of potential GDP.
4. As a percentage of household disposable income.
5. As a percentage of GDP.
Source: OECD (2016), OECD Economic Outlook: Statistics and Projections (database); Australian Bureau of Statistics.

There are several risks to this central scenario with implications for potential output and productivity:

● Trade-related uncertainties are a key element in Australia's risk profile. Developments in global demand and prices for iron ore and coal will be critical, particularly demand for these commodities in China (Figure 10). Aggregate demand in China is also of growing importance for Australia's trade in services, notably in tourism as China's middle class grows.

● Non-commodity investment growth may not pick up as expected. Capital-expenditure and non-residential building-approval data have yet to show a clear positive trend (Figure 11). However, business-credit growth has been picking up, potentially signalling stronger investment ahead (see discussion below).

Figure 10. **China is Australia's largest trading partner**

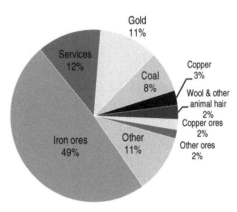

A. Exports by partners, 2015-16

B. Exports to China by item, 2015

Source: Australian Department of Foreign Affairs and Trade.

StatLink 🔗 *http://dx.doi.org/10.1787/888933456717*

Figure 11. **Non-commodity investment has yet to pick up**

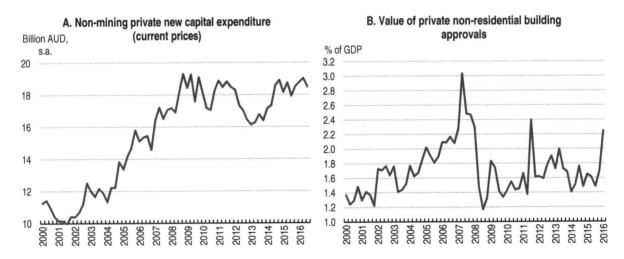

A. Non-mining private new capital expenditure (current prices)

B. Value of private non-residential building approvals

Source: ABS (2016), 5625.0 – Private New Capital Expenditure and Expected Expenditure; ABS (2016), 8731.0 – Building Approvals; OECD (2016), Analytical Database.

StatLink 🔗 *http://dx.doi.org/10.1787/888933456725*

● Shifts in US monetary policy, uncertainties about Brexit, rising protectionism and revisions to China's exchange rate policy, may catalyse global exchange-rate volatility that could affect Australia's trade.

Indicators suggest there is some risk of downturn (Box 2), with several potentially destabilising events possible (Table 2). Threats to stability from overheating in terms of output or inflation has lessened in recent years (Figure 12, Panel A). However, macro-financial indicators underline the threat from the housing market, with house prices and related indicators (house indebtedness, bank size, Figure 12, Panel B) pointing to continued vulnerability. Any impact will most likely be through aggregate demand than financial instability. Although there are a number of factors likely to mitigate the systemic impact of these vulnerabilities, including large aggregate mortgage prepayment buffers and recently tightened macro-prudential measures, a fall in house prices and or demand could have significant macroeconomic implications. Specifically, the market may not ease gently but develop into a rout on prices and demand with significant macroeconomic implications. Externally, Australia, as always, is exposed to the vagaries of global commodity markets and this might include a renewed plunge in prices (or, positively, a strong resurgence). Australia's iron ore production is among the lowest cost in the world and therefore comparatively insulated from such developments, however its coal sector is relatively

Figure 12. **Macro-financial vulnerabilities have eased since the global financial crisis**

Deviations of indicators from their real time long-term averages (0), with the highest deviations representing the greatest potential vulnerability (+1), and the lowest deviations representing the smallest potential vulnerability (-1)[1]

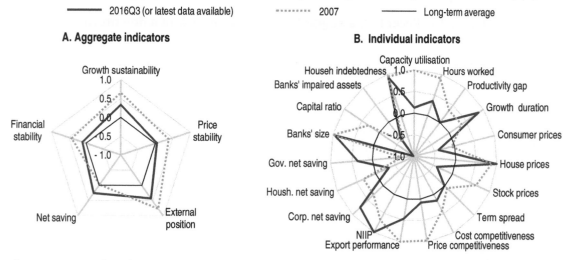

1. Each aggregate macro-financial vulnerability indicator is calculated by aggregating (simple average) normalised individual indicators. Growth sustainability includes: capacity utilisation, total hours worked as a proportion of the working-age population (hours worked), difference between GDP growth and productivity growth (productivity gap), and an indicator combining the length and strength of expansion from the previous trough (growth duration). Price stability includes: headline and core inflation (consumer prices), the average of house prices-to-rent ratio and house prices-to-income ratio (house prices), stock market index (ASX200) adjusted by nominal GDP (stock prices), and the difference between long-term and short-term government bond interest rates (term spread). External position includes: the average of unit labour cost based real effective exchange rate (REER), and consumer price based REER (cost competitiveness), relative prices of exported goods and services (price competitiveness), ratio of exports to export markets (export performance) and net international investment position (NIIP) as a percentage of GDP. Net saving includes: government, household and corporate net saving, all expressed as a percentage of GDP. Financial stability includes: size of banking sector as a percentage of GDP, Tier 1 capital ratio, banks' impaired facilities to loans and advances, and household debt-to-disposable income ratio.

Source: OECD calculations based on OECD (2017), OECD Economic Outlook: Statistics and Projections (database); Australian Bureau of Statistics; Reserve Bank of Australia; Australian Prudential Regulation Authority; Thomson Reuters Datastream.

StatLink ⧉ http://dx.doi.org/10.1787/888933456737

Box 2. **Predicting downturn in the Australian economy using the OECD's resilience database**

The OECD's database of vulnerability indicators (Hermansen and Röhn 2015; Röhn et al., 2015) can be used to assess the risk of downturn. The database comprises over 70 indicators across six categories of vulnerability (five domestic, one international). Echoing a number of recent *Surveys* (e.g. 2016 *Economic Survey* of the United States), statistical methods can be used to develop leading indicators of past downturns and recessions.

Four downturns (not all are recessions as they do not fulfil the usual definition of at least two consecutive quarters of falling output) were identified for Australia in the period spanned by the resilience data (which begin in the mid-1970s). Principal components analysis was used to develop a single-number leading indicator. The most powerful elements proved to be those in the category of "spillovers, contagion and global risks", such as global asset market prices and global credit growth. This fits in with Australia's strong linkage to global markets. The leading indicator was then used to estimate the downturn probability at different time horizons (Figure 13).

As similar exercises for other countries have found, the indicator developed from the resilience database is not very accurate. It predicts two of Australia's four previous downturn events quite well (in Figure 13, the indicators are performing well if they peak around the beginning of a downturn). However it does not predict the second downturn and flags problems in the run up to the global financial crisis but is inaccurate on the timing.

Bearing in mind the limited accuracy, the emergence of peaks in the most recent data suggests there is a non-negligible risk of downturn.

Figure 13. **Recent data suggest there is some risk of a downturn**
In-sample downturn probabilities, 3 components

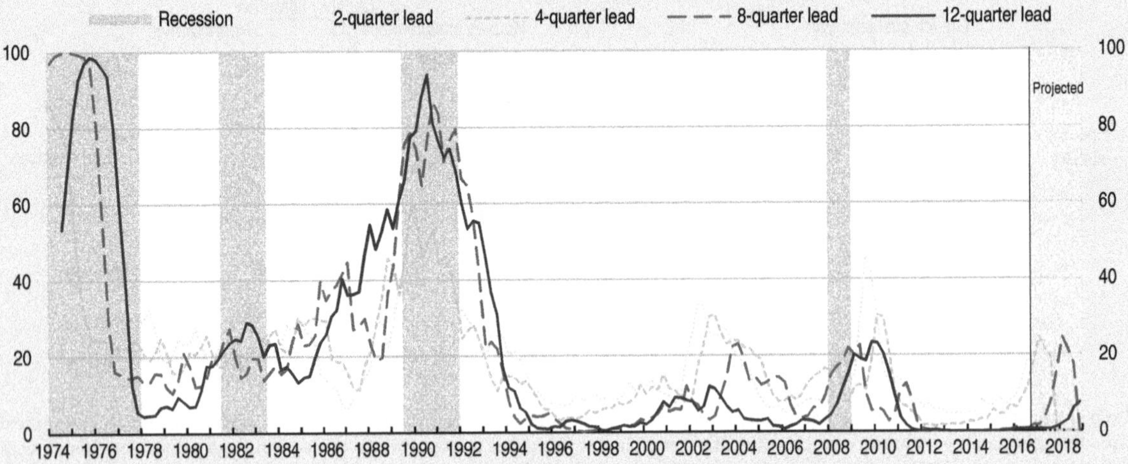

Source: OECD calculations.

StatLink http://dx.doi.org/10.1787/888933456745

Table 2. **Extreme vulnerabilities for the Australian economy**

Vulnerability	Possible outcome
Dramatic house-price correction	A large drop off in house prices could cut household consumption and increase mortgage defaults
Renewed plunge in global iron ore and coal prices	Further cost-savings and retrenchment of investment among mining companies with impact on jobs and incomes

more exposed as its production is distributed across the cost curve. Interaction of downside scenarios is likely to exacerbate the negative macroeconomic outcomes. For instance, a negative external shock could lift unemployment sharply which would result in significant fall in consumption and rising mortgage stress and falling house prices.

The economy is well positioned to handle shocks such as those described in Table 2. The speed and strength of the rebalancing processes in response to the end of the commodity boom auger well for the economy's shock-absorbing capacity. In addition, Australia has more reserve capacity for monetary and fiscal stimulus than many other OECD economies (see discussion below).

Monetary and financial-market policy: coping with low interest rates

As in many other economies, monetary policy has been the principal tool for supporting aggregate demand in recent years. This partly reflects that fiscal policy has focused on curbing deficits following the large fiscal expansion during the global financial crisis and consequent rise in public debt (Figure 14). Monetary stimulus has been consistent with the RBA's medium-term inflation target band of 2% to 3% (Figure 7), as inflation has been low, and interest rates are higher in Australia than in the United States or the euro area (Figure 14).

Unless downside risks materialise, the current supportive stance of monetary policy remains appropriate at present, particularly in the absence of inflationary pressures. However, a side effect is a risk that accommodative policy may be increasingly distorting financial markets and, especially, house prices (which have risen to very high levels). Eventually, rates will need to be normalised, but the timing and pace will depend on developments in growth, employment, inflation, and the housing market.

Macro-prudential measures are helping contain housing-loan growth

House prices and household debt have reached unprecedented highs (Figure 15), in part because policy-rate cuts have lowered debt servicing costs (most housing loans are set at variable interest rates). In real terms, house prices have increased by 250% since the mid-1990s. Furthermore, the ratio of house prices to incomes has undergone further increase in recent years, straining affordability, especially for first-time buyers in Sydney. Foreign demand for housing, while a contributing factor, does not appear to have had a substantial impact on price growth. There are signs that the housing market is cooling. Recent data indicate price growth has eased in most urban centres, reflecting in part a substantial supply response – dwelling approvals and investments have increased substantially in recent years (Figure 15). However, the significant increase in Australia's house prices and price to income ratios remains. A continued rise of the market, fuelled by both investor and owner-occupier demand, may end in a significant downward correction that spreads to the rest of the economy.

Figure 14. **Monetary policy remains accommodative, while fiscal deficits are declining**

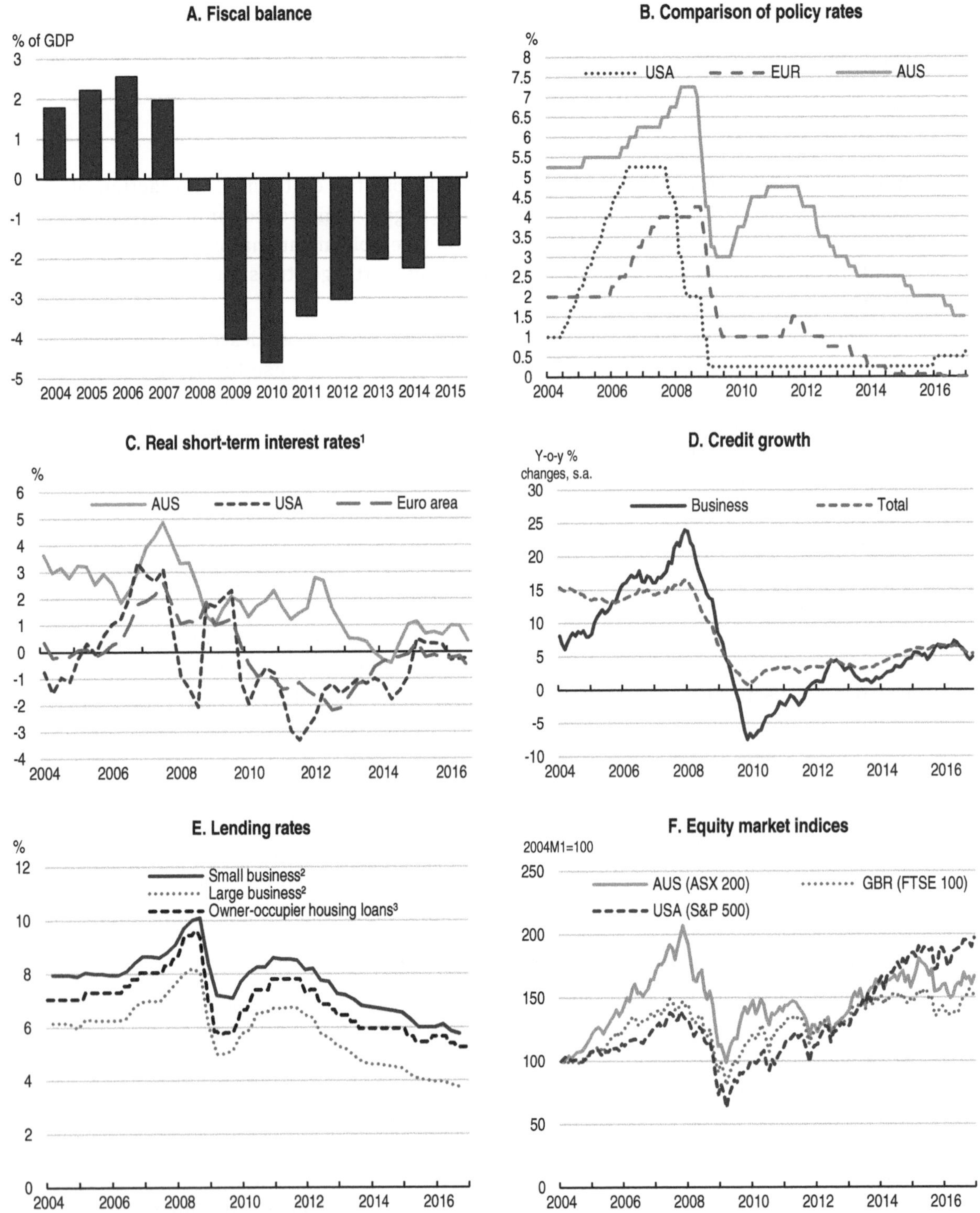

A. Fiscal balance

B. Comparison of policy rates

C. Real short-term interest rates[1]

D. Credit growth

E. Lending rates

F. Equity market indices

1. Average three-month money market rate adjusted by CPI.
2. Weighted-average rate on credit outstanding.
3. "Standard" rates which apply to housing loans with facilities such as the option to redraw or make early repayments.
Source: Reserve Bank of Australia (2016); OECD (2016), OECD Analytical Database; Thomson Reuters.

StatLink 🔗 *http://dx.doi.org/10.1787/888933456752*

Figure 15. **Housing market indicators show hints of a slowdown**

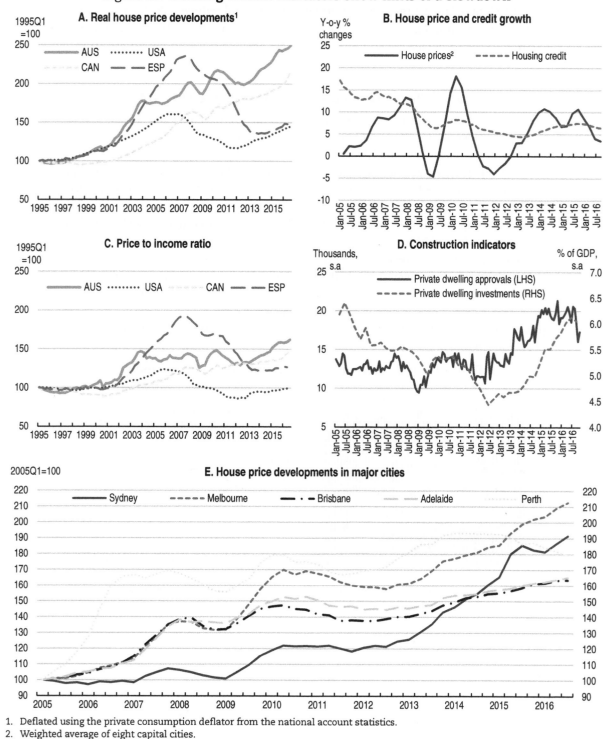

1. Deflated using the private consumption deflator from the national account statistics.
2. Weighted average of eight capital cities.

Source: OECD (2017), OECD Analytical House Price database; ABS, 8731.0 – Building Approvals, Australia; ABS, 5206.0 Australian National Accounts: National Income, Expenditure and Product; Reserve Bank of Australia; ABS, 6416.0 – Residential Property Price Indexes: Eight Capital Cities, Sep 2016.

StatLink ᴍꜱᴾ *http://dx.doi.org/10.1787/888933456768*

As recommended in the previous *Survey* (OECD, 2014a), the authorities have deployed "macro-prudential" measures to cool mortgage lending and reduce risks (Box 3). Measures include pressure on banks to limit growth of mortgage lending to those purchasing for investment purposes (see Table 3 and Annex, below). These augment institution-by-

---

Box 3. **The macroprudential measures taken in 2014**

In response to concerns about the level of risk being taken on by banks and households, the Australian Prudential Regulation Authority (APRA) announced measures in December 2014 to reinforce sound housing lending practices (APRA, 2014). These measures focus on:

- the extent of higher-risk mortgage lending – for example, high loan-to-income loans, high loan-to-valuation (LVR) loans, interest-only loans to owner occupiers, and loans with very long terms

- the pace of growth in investor housing lending – in particular portfolio growth materially above a threshold of 10 %

- interest rate buffers and floors used in loan serviceability assessments – in APRA's view, these should incorporate an interest rate buffer of at least 2 % above the loan product rate, and a floor lending rate of at least 7 %, when assessing borrowers' ability to service their loans.

These measures, coupled with increased mortgage risk weights for Internal Rating Based (IRB) banks (i.e used by major banks), have seen investor credit growth slow and an improvement in the quality of credit being extended in the mortgage market (Figure 16).

Figure 16. **Indicators of costs and risks in housing credit**

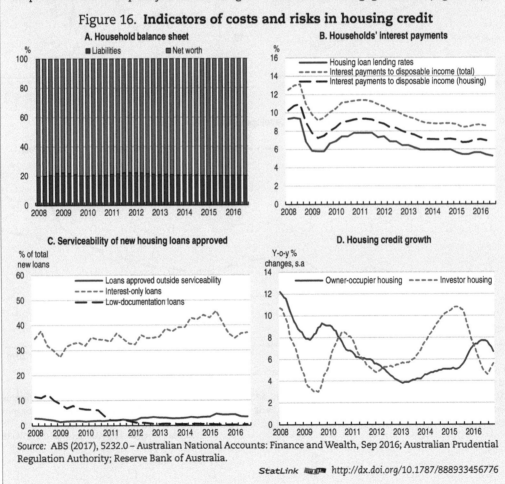

Source: ABS (2017), 5232.0 – Australian National Accounts: Finance and Wealth, Sep 2016; Australian Prudential Regulation Authority; Reserve Bank of Australia.

StatLink ⟪⟫ http://dx.doi.org/10.1787/888933456776

Table 3. **Past OECD recommendations on monetary and financial stability**

Topic and summary of recommendations	Summary of action taken since 2014 *Survey*
Improve the functioning of the housing market	
Continue intensive monitoring of the housing market; maintain deep micro-prudential oversight and consider using macro-prudential tools to bolster credit safeguards and signal concern	Use of macro-prudential measures has begun (alongside continued deep micro-prudential oversight). For instance, investor lending by banks has been limited to 10% growth annually
Facilitate housing supply in particular through planning-regulation reform at state and territory level	State-level planning-regulation reform continues
Examine competition and credit issues in the financial sector	
Reduce banking sector privileges. Consider reducing banks' implicit guarantees, tackling risk-weighting advantages in mortgage lending, improving credit databases	Risk weightings on mortgage lending were raised in July 2015 for banks that use the internal ratings-based models

institution scrutiny of mortgage lending ("micro-prudential" policy), which in the Australian context is an effective approach because the four major banks account for a large share of mortgage lending (around 80% in the first quarter of 2016 according to data published by the banking regulator, APRA). Demand-side measures, such as macro-prudential tools, should continue to play a role with careful attention to distributional consequences for households. As recommended in past *Surveys* (Table 3), supply-side measures, including planning-regulation reform, can also help ease market pressure over the longer term.

Resilience and competition issues in banking

The global financial crisis did not lead to systemic bank failures in Australia but, as elsewhere, prompted tighter regulation and alteration in banking practices. Banks have shifted their funding composition away from short-term debt and towards deposits (Figure 17). Furthermore, a recent report by the banking regulator (APRA, 2016) indicates that capital ratios have reached the thresholds recommended by the Financial System Inquiry ("Murray Inquiry") (Australian Government, 2014). However, APRA's report notes that banks must continue increasing their capital ratios to at least maintain, if not improve, their relative positioning. The Murray Inquiry underscored that strengthening bank resilience should also include new measures to limit the costs to the public in the event of bank failure. Specifically, it recommended the establishment of a loss absorbing and recapitalisation framework in line with international developments to allow effective resolution with limited risk to taxpayer funds. This approach has been endorsed by the government and APRA is developing detailed implementation.

The Murray Inquiry's call for stronger resilience also reflects concerns that four major banks have substantial market share in many financial services (especially retail services), an issue that has been raised in previous *Surveys*. Bolstering resilience can reduce the banks' implicit guarantees, which put them in an advantageous position in providing financial services. Concern about the strength of banking regulation has prompted efforts to identify and eliminate advantages for banks in regulatory technicalities. On this front, there has been welcome progress with the reduction in major banks' advantages over other lenders that use the standardised model of risk assessment in the mortgage market arising from differences in mortgage risk weights (see Table 3).

Figure 17. **Banking-sector resilience is being bolstered**

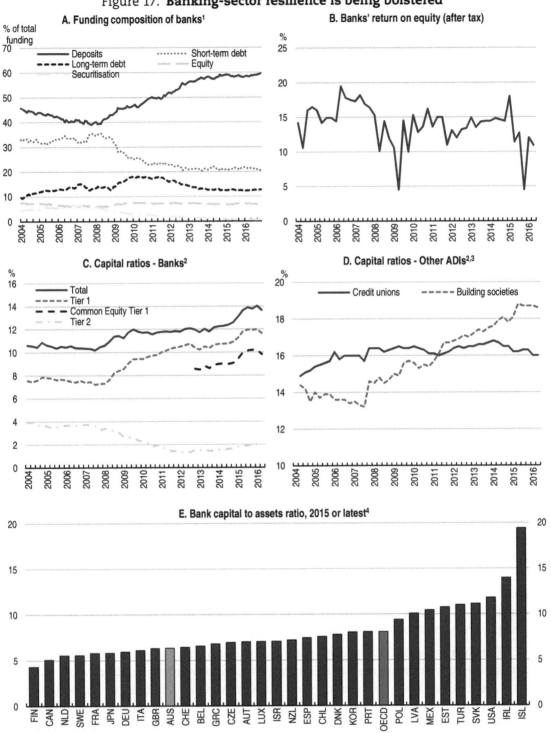

1. Short-term debt and long-term debt are adjusted for movements in foreign exchange rates. Short-term debt includes deposits and intragroup funding from non-residents.
2. Percentage of risk-weighted assets; break in March 2008 due to introduction of Basel II for most ADIs; break in March 2013 due to the introduction of Basel III for all ADIs.
3. ADI refers to an authorised deposit-taking institution, meaning a body corporate authorised under section 9 of the Act, to carry on banking business in Australia (e.g. a bank, building society or credit union).
4. The ratio of bank capital and reserves to total assets, which are not risk weighted.
Source: Australian Prudential Regulation Authority; Reserve Bank of Australia; World Bank.

StatLink ᴹⁱˢᵖ *http://dx.doi.org/10.1787/888933456789*

Fiscal consolidation, tax and spending reform

Compared with other OECD countries, Australia's tax burden, public spending and public debt are low (Figure 18). Following the global financial crisis, the authorities provided timely fiscal support that helped Australia avoid a recession (one of the few OECD countries to do so). Since then the fiscal deficit has been unwinding, though somewhat slowly (Table 4 and Figure 19). The federal deficit in financial year 2015-16 was 2.4% of GDP, which is below its peak of 4.2% but not low enough to bring a fall in the debt-GDP ratio.

Australian fiscal policy is guided by a broad rule of achieving a balanced budget (or surpluses) in the federal budget "over the cycle". State governments do not substantially affect the overall fiscal stance because their balances are comparatively small. The current government has adopted an operational goal of reaching a federal budget surplus of 1% of GDP "as soon as possible" (Australian Government, 2016a), which is more than sufficient to put the debt-GDP ratio on a downward track. Simulations suggest that a budget surplus of 1% after 2021-22 would bring the ratio to 25% of GDP by 2025-26 and close to zero by 2040 (Figure 20). Australia's balanced-budget/surplus guidance reflects a longstanding preference for achieving low debt burdens.

Figure 18. **Government expenditure, taxation and public-debt are comparatively low**

As a percentage of GDP[1]

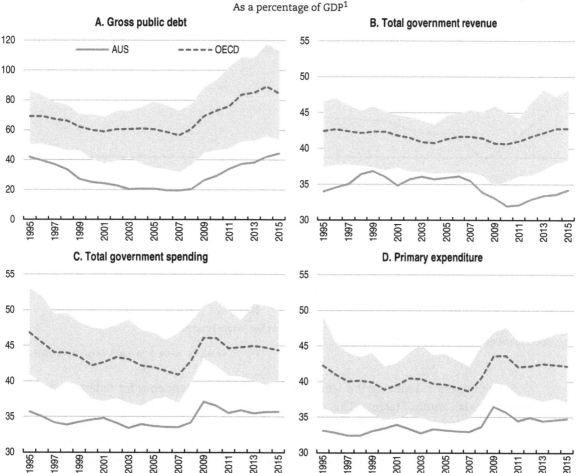

1. Data represent general-government accounts (i.e. including sub-national government accounts). The shaded area denotes the 25th to 75th percentile range of available data for OECD countries. OECD is a simple average of data for available countries.

Source: OECD (2016), OECD Analytical Database.

StatLink ⟨⟩ http://dx.doi.org/10.1787/888933456791

Table 4. **Fiscal indicators**
Per cent of GDP

	2013	2014	2015	2016[1]	2017[1]	2018[1]
Spending and revenue						
Total revenue	33.6	33.4	33.9	33.8	34.0	34.1
Total expenditure	35.6	35.7	35.7	36.4	36.1	35.7
Net interest payments	0.6	0.7	0.6	0.6	0.6	0.6
Budget balance						
Fiscal balance	-2.0	-2.3	-1.8	-2.6	-2.0	-1.5
Cyclically adjusted fiscal balance[2]	-1.2	-1.4	-0.8	-1.7	-1.2	-1.1
Underlying fiscal balance[2]	-1.5	-1.5	-1.5	-1.8	-1.2	-1.1
Underlying primary fiscal balance[2]	-0.9	-0.8	-0.9	-1.3	-0.7	-0.5
Federal budget balance[3]	-1.2	-3.1	-2.4	-2.4	-	-
Public debt						
Gross debt	38.3	42.3	44.5	45.4	45.1	44.6
Net debt	-15.4	-13.1	-14.4	-11.4	-8.9	-6.9

1. Projections.
2. Per cent of potential GDP. The underlying balances are adjusted for the cycle and for one-offs. For more details, see OECD Economic Outlook Sources and Methods.
3. "Underlying cash balance", which equals to receipts less payments, less net Future Fund earnings. Fiscal year basis (i.e. 2015 data refer to 2014-15).
Source: OECD (2016), OECD Economic Outlook: Statistics and Projections (database); Government of Australia, Budget papers.

Figure 19. **Consolidation in the federal-government budget**
Federal budget balance[1]

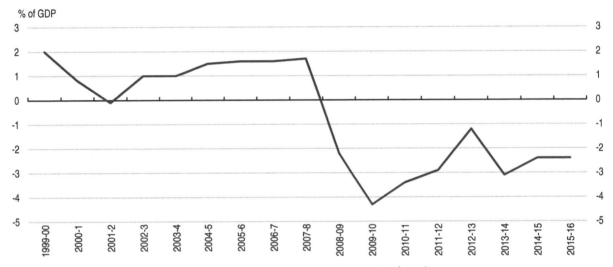

1. "Underlying cash balance", which equals receipts less payments, less net Future Fund earnings.
Source: Government of Australia, Budget papers.

StatLink ⬛ http://dx.doi.org/10.1787/888933456802

Slow progress in reducing the federal deficit reflects the tendency for federal budget outcomes to fall short of targets. This is despite active measures and consolidation due to bracket creep. Personal income tax thresholds are not automatically indexed in Australia; which provides leeway for discretionary adjustment of the tax schedule as part of structural reforms. Discretion on threshold updating may also serve, at times questionably, to help resolve budget imbalances. The weak pace of consolidation in large part reflects disappointing nominal GDP growth. Also, some policy initiatives have involved sizeable multi-year spending commitments, including a lift in the base-rate of the pension and

Figure 20. **Under the government's operational goal the debt-to-GDP ratio will be put on a downward track**

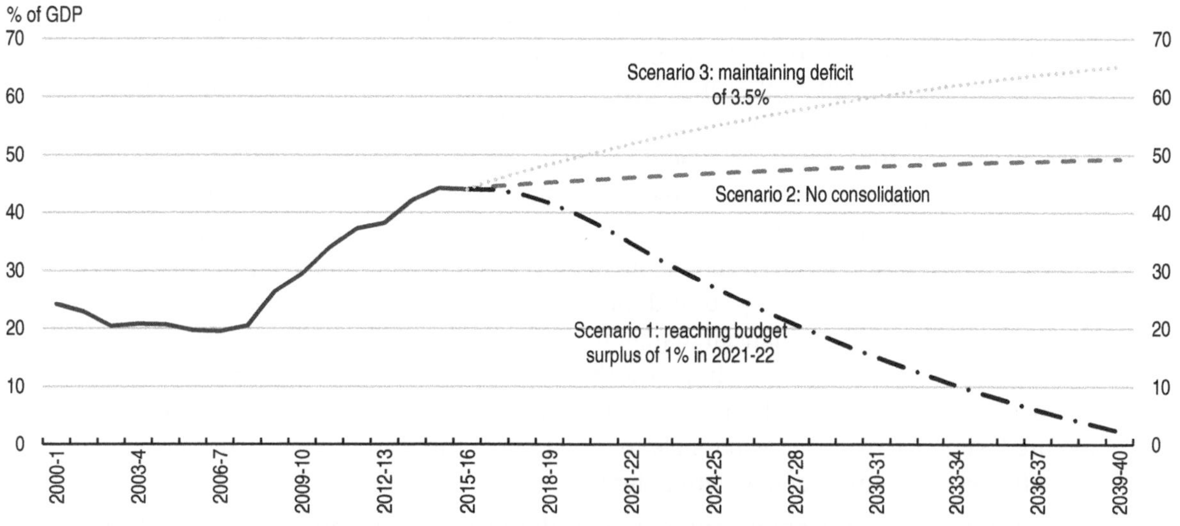

% of GDP
70
60
50
40
30
20
10
0
Scenario 3: maintaining deficit of 3.5%
Scenario 2: No consolidation
Scenario 1: reaching budget surplus of 1% in 2021-22
2000-1
2003-4
2006-7
2009-10
2012-13
2015-16
2018-19
2021-22
2024-25
2027-28
2030-31
2033-34
2036-37
2039-40

Note: These debt projections use a simple model that uses various deficit trajectories and projection of GDP growth to calculate debt-to-GDP ratios looking forward. The model does not explicitly incorporate the channels of interaction between deficit profiles and GDP, nor structural influences on deficit developments and GDP growth, such as the impact of population ageing.

Source: OECD calculations based on OECD Analytical Database and Government of Australia.

StatLink http://dx.doi.org/10.1787/888933456819

increased commitments on hospitals and schools funding. Such commitments have meant spending as a share of GDP has remained above pre-crisis levels (Figure 21). Over the next few years, spending commitments will be boosted by the ongoing implementation of a reform of support systems for the disabled (the National Disability Insurance Scheme, NDIS, see below) and higher defence spending.

Figure 21. **Increases in public spending compared with pre-crisis levels**

Additional general government expenses by purpose as a share of GDP, relative to the levels of 2007-8

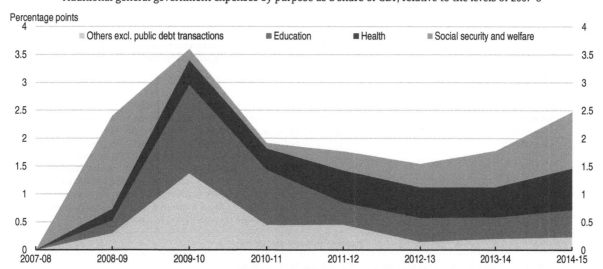

Percentage points
4
3.5
3
2.5
2
1.5
1
0.5
0
Others excl. public debt transactions
Education
Health
Social security and welfare
2007-08
2008-09
2009-10
2010-11
2011-12
2012-13
2013-14
2014-15

Source: ABS (2016), 5512.0 – Government Finance Statistics, Australia, 2014-15.

StatLink http://dx.doi.org/10.1787/888933456824

Australia's fiscal position is strong and the current fiscal stance is appropriate given the outlook. According to a recent cross-country study (Fall and Fournier, 2015), debt could begin reducing output growth between 70-90% of GDP. This implies Australia, with gross debt at 44%, still has a significant margin to absorb shocks and actively stimulate growth. Indeed, the government could run a substantially larger deficit for some time without coming close to the limits suggested above (Figure 20). In this context, should the downside risks materialise, the authorities should actively use fiscal policy to support the economy, as they did in 2008-09. The more financial and global the shock, and the closer monetary policy is to the zero-lower bound, the stronger the case for using fiscal policy, particularly if the exchange-rate does not respond. Though fiscal stimulus would delay the return to a balanced budget and raise public debt, it would be unlikely to jeopardise fiscal sustainability or generate financial market turmoil. Moreover, it would take some pressure off expansionary monetary policy and thereby reduce the risk of financial market distortions. Automatic stabilisers should be allowed to operate. Additional stimulus, if required, should look as far as possible to investments that can be quickly dispersed and also lift aggregate supply and growth potential.

The ramping up of spending commitments during the commodity boom suggests that medium-term fiscal discipline could benefit from a spending ceiling or a longer-term debt anchor (as suggested in recent IMF analysis). This could help guide the use of fiscal space and provide a guard against Australia's longstanding vulnerability to excessive fiscal expansion during commodity booms. An alternative, or additional, approach would be to institute federal- and state-level stabilisation funds (or make greater use of existing funds, such as the Future Fund), as recommended in previous *Surveys* (see Table 5, below), and following the approach of some other commodity producers (such as Alberta (Canada), Chile, and Norway).

Table 5. **Past OECD recommendations on maintaining fiscal prudence and ensuring efficient tax and public spending**

Topic and summary of recommendations	Summary of action taken since 2014 *Survey*
Strengthen mechanism that aid fiscal discipline	
Prioritise medium-term fiscal consolidation to rebuild fiscal buffers in light of Australia's exposure to external risk. Consider establishing a stabilisation fund	Federal budget consolidation remains ambitious, deficit outcomes have fallen short of goals. No progress has been made in widening the use of stabilisation funds
Tax reform	
Rebalance the tax mix; shift away from income and transaction taxes Make greater use of efficient tax bases such as the Goods and Services Tax and land tax	Tax measures in the 2016-17 budget envisage further reduction in the rate of corporate tax and further measures to combat base erosion and profit shifting in corporate taxation (see Table 6). The Government has added GST to the online purchase of digital products and service and is introducing legislation to add GST to low-value imported goods. As regards making greater use of land tax (and less use of inefficient taxes), so far only one jurisdiction, Australian Capital Territory, has embarked on a major reform. The reform is increasing land taxes, reducing transfer duties on conveyances and abolishing insurance taxes
Improving the federal-state system	
Reform state financing: reduce grant conditionality further, instigate state-level tax reforms to enhance funding autonomy Address federal-state responsibilities: improve co-ordination and co-operation and in health care in particular, consider a reallocation of responsibilities	No major initiative

Improving the tax system

Taxation has been receiving welcome policy attention. The tax mix remains tilted towards direct taxes, especially on corporates, that can hurt growth. Measures addressing this issue form part of the tax reforms that are a central theme of the current government's economic policy. Detailed measures were outlined in the 2016-17 Budget proposals (Table 6), the elements of most structural significance are:

● Corporate income tax rate cuts (as part of the "Ten Year Enterprise Tax Plan"), initially for small businesses with eventual extension to all businesses. Australia's standard rate of corporate tax is 30%, which is high in international comparison. Proposals also include an increased tax discount for unincorporated small business.

● Further measures to combat corporate tax avoidance, including the establishment of a tax avoidance taskforce.

● A superannuation reform package, comprising reduced tax concessions for high-income earners and more generous tax treatment for low income earners.

However, the tax system could be improved in some respects:

● There has been no progress on a major tax reform that makes greater use of value added tax (the Goods and Services Tax, GST) and little progress in land-tax reform, both moves long recommended in OECD *Surveys* and discussed widely in Australia (Figure 22). As GST revenues are currently passed to the states, such reform would require some reshaping of federal-state financial arrangements. To the extent the Australian GST is less progressive compared to the personal-income taxes, reform would also need to address poverty and income distribution issues, perhaps by adjusting welfare policies.

Table 6. **Selected tax measures proposed in the 2016-17 Budget**

"Ten-year Enterprise Tax Plan"	Key details
Corporate income tax rate cuts led by further cuts for small business	The overall goal is reduction of the corporate tax rate (currently 30% for large business and 28.5% for small business) to 25% over 10 years. The process will include further cuts in the concessionary rate for small-businesses along with progressive increases in the cut-off threshold for eligibility to the concessionary rate, until it applies to all businesses
Increased Tax Discount for small business	For unincorporated small businesses eligibility for the tax discount will be expanded to those businesses with turnover less than AUD 5 million (compared to AUD 2 million currently) and increased to 8% (compared to 5% currently) for the 2016-17 income year. The discount will increase over time, in line with reductions in the corporate tax rate, from 8% to 16% 2026-27

"Tax integrity" measures	
Superannuation Reform Package	Legislation to implement a suite of reforms to better target the superannuation tax concessions, and improve the flexibility and integrity of the superannuation system has passed parliament. This includes: ● Caps on transfers into the retirement phase of the superannuation system under concessional tax arrangements ● Lower ceilings on tax concessions in the contribution phase ● Introduction of a new tax offset in pensions (the Low Income Superannuation Tax Offset) ● Tax deductions for personal superannuation contributions
Corporate tax integrity measures	● Establishment of a tax avoidance taskforce ● Introduction of a diverted profits tax ● Amending Australia's transfer pricing rules to give effect to the OECD's transfer pricing recommendations ● Stronger protection for tax whistle-blowers ● Further measures to close loopholes in tax arrangements under the consolidation regime ● Implementation of the OECD's hybrid mismatch rules to reduce multinationals' exploitation of differences in tax treatment across jurisdictions

Figure 22. **The standard rate of Goods and Services Tax is low in international comparison**

Standard rates of Value Added Tax/Goods and Services Tax, 2016

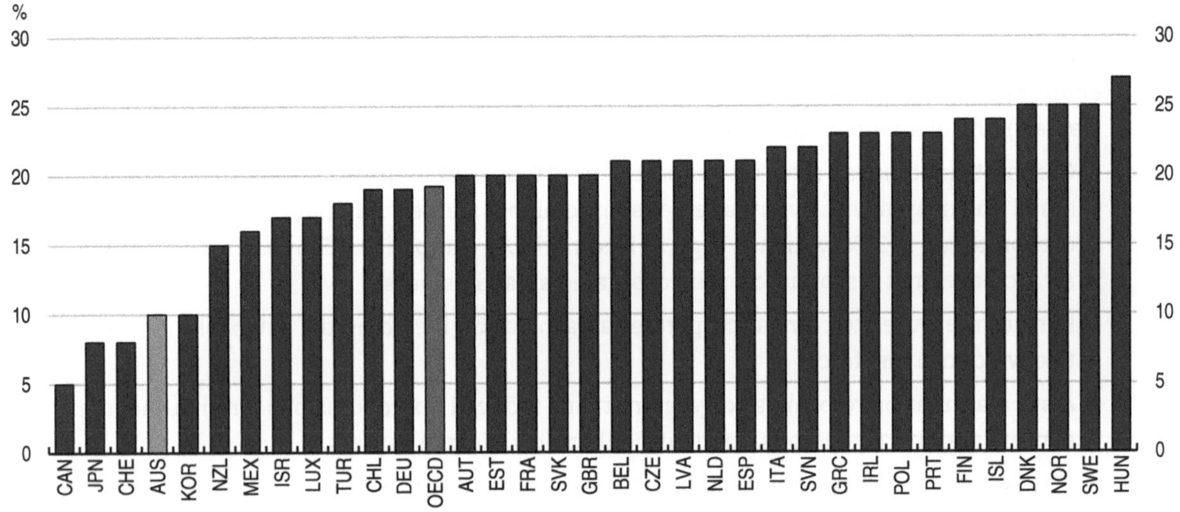

Source: OECD Tax Database.

StatLink ⫘⫘ http://dx.doi.org/10.1787/888933456837

- State level taxation still involves a number of inefficiencies and distortions, particularly heavy use of transactions taxes in real estate (greater use of recurrent taxes on residential property would be preferable), substantial exemptions in payroll taxes and a multitude of small-scale charges and fees. Replacing these inefficient taxes with a higher GST and greater use of land tax, for example, would improve economic performance. In Australian Capital Territory a substantial shift away from inefficient taxes towards land tax is underway but progress in other jurisdictions is limited (see Table 5 and Annex).

Efficiency enhancing reforms in public expenditure

Continued efforts to innovate economies and to find efficiency gains in public spending could strengthen public finances, raise the quality of public services and increase the effectiveness of welfare and transfer payments. Government spending should, in addition, be redirected towards additional public investments with substantial long-term returns, particularly economic infrastructure that is partnered with the private-sector (Figure 23). To ensure long-term returns, cost-benefit analysis should play a prominent role in project selection.

As detailed in Chapter 1 of this *Survey*, alterations to the public procurement system are planned that widen the field of prospective bidders to bring more innovative solutions to public service provision. Additional steps could, for instance, include further shifts to outcome rather than output criteria, thus providing greater leeway on how services are delivered. Further development of digital government services could also help. In addition, making public data more widely available for commercial and research use could support more general research and development.

Support for small and medium enterprises (SMEs) should also be scrutinised (Chapter 1). Australia has around 340 innovation-related schemes, most aimed at SMEs. Strong review and reform mechanisms are important, as is making firms aware of the available support. Size-based policies, by definition, involve cut-off points that can

Figure 23. **Australia's government investment is below the OECD average**

Government investment as a share of GDP, 2015 or latest

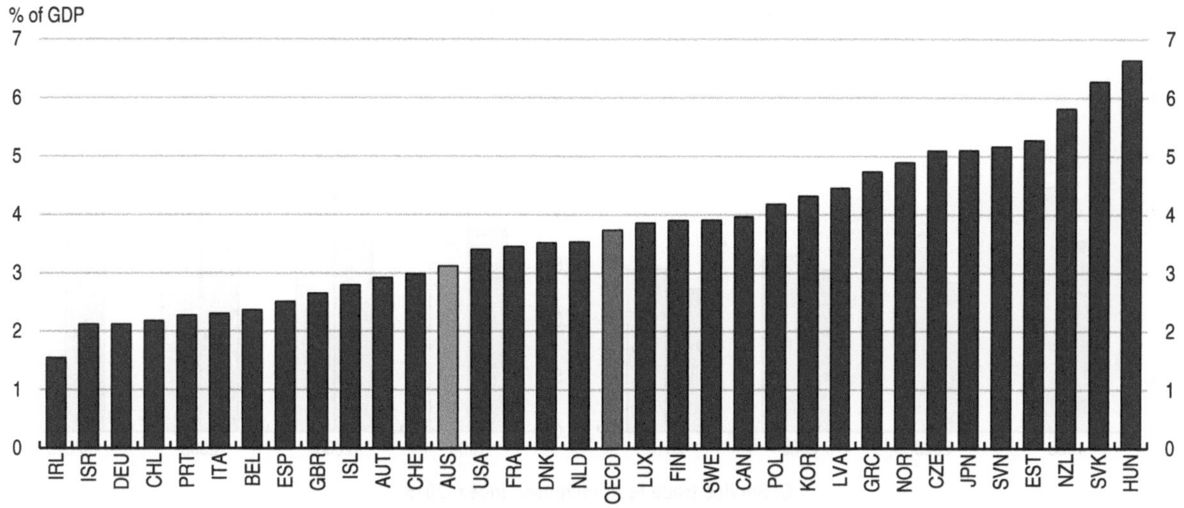

Source: OECD (2016), OECD Analytical Database; OECD (2016), OECD Government at a Glance (database).

StatLink ᵐˢᵖ *http://dx.doi.org/10.1787/888933456847*

dissuade firms from transitioning to larger scales of operation. With the current government adding more size-based support (in tax as well as subsidies), the risk of distortions and inefficiencies may become substantial. In addition, Australia has a track record of prolonged subsidies for "sunset" industries or for new production facilities in economically deprived areas. The termination of subsidies on car production plants in Australia removed one of the most prominent and longstanding examples. However, the authorities continue to resort to industry subsidy.

Encouraging business productivity and innovation through framework conditions

Progress in structural reform in recent decades has significantly improved policy settings for the business environment on many fronts. However, as other countries have been improving their settings, Australia's advantage has been eroded (Figure 24). This *Survey*'s in-depth chapters highlight the importance of more intensive generation and adoption of innovation for future productivity growth, issues which are also prominent in the government's *National Innovation and Science Agenda* (NISA, see Box 4). The *Agenda* endeavours to make a number of incremental changes which, together, can make a significant change.

Improving framework conditions to boost innovative capacity

Rapid and widespread assimilation of advances in the global frontiers of know-how and technologies are key to sustaining high productivity. This process can be substantially bolstered by efficient resource allocation and competitive markets as this boosts the number of businesses operating at, or close to, these frontiers. Chapter 1 underscores the importance of the following:

● Continued follow up on the Competition Policy Review (the "Harper Review", Australian Government, 2015b).

Figure 24. **Australia's advantage in lighter regulations has been eroded**

OECD indicators on product market regulation, employment protection legislation and service trade restrictiveness index

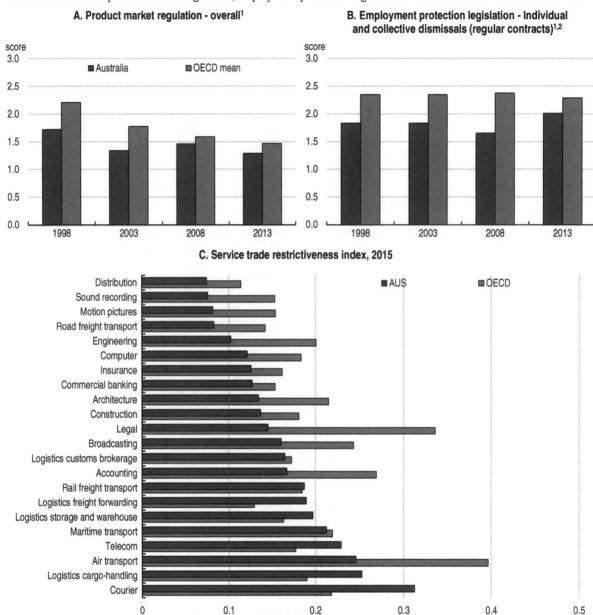

1. Scores potentially range from zero to 6 and increase with restrictiveness.
2. Weighted sum of sub-indicators concerning the regulations for individual dismissals (weight of 5/7) and additional provisions for collective dismissals (2/7).

Source: OECD (2015), "Economy-wide regulation", OECD Product Market Regulation Statistics (database); OECD/IAB, Employment Protection Database, 2013 update; OECD (2015), Services Trade Restrictiveness Index.

StatLink ⬛⬛⬛ *http://dx.doi.org/10.1787/888933456854*

- Reducing barriers to labour mobility. Large distances between major urban centres make labour mobility more costly and aggravate skill mismatch. Further reduction in labour-market frictions generated by interstate differences in education and vocational qualifications would help, as would measures that assist household mobility. Reduced skill mismatch can also improve job opportunities and reducing unemployment; a "win-win" measure in inclusiveness and productivity.

> ## Box 4. **The National Science and Innovation Agenda**
>
> The *National Innovation and Science Agenda* (NISA) was announced on the 7th of December, 2015. The Agenda is built on four pillars:
>
> - *Culture and capital*: focuses on rewarding entrepreneurialism and supporting innovative start-ups by improving the availability of finance. Initiatives include tax treatments to encourage small businesses to take risks and innovate. Working in partnership with the private sector, the government has established the CSIRO Innovation Fund and the Biomedical Translation Fund to back high potential ideas.
>
> - *Collaboration*: seeks to incentivise greater collaboration through changes to university funding formulas, providing investment in research infrastructure and an introduction of a national impact and engagement assessment framework.
>
> - *Talent and skills*: aims to support young Australians to create and use digital technologies, expanding opportunities for women in the field of Science, Technology, Engineering and Mathematics and encouraging more entrepreneurial and research talent from overseas.
>
> - *Government as an exemplar*: commits the public sector to lead by example in becoming more innovative in how services are delivered and how public data should be shared. Also part of this, the government has established Innovation and Science Australia as an independent advisory board responsible for researching planning and advising the Government on all science, research, and innovation matters.
>
> The authorities have implemented, or are on track to implement, all measures in the first wave of NISA. Also, the second and third waves of NISA have been outlined, which will focus on new ways of attracting private sector investment and infrastructure for science and simplify the way businesses interact with government by removing unnecessary regulatory measures.
>
> More information can be found at *http://innovation.gov.au*.

- Encouraging a positive process of "creative destruction" through firm entry and exit, as this keeps more businesses closer to knowledge frontiers. Past reforms have reduced the regulatory burdens for establishing a business. Regarding firm exit, proposals to lighten insolvency regulation as part of the NISA reform are encouraging. Barriers to firm growth may also be an issue; SME support policies can inadvertently create disincentives to growth beyond a certain size, for instance.

- Working towards intellectual property (IP) arrangements that provide incentives to innovate and allow access to knowledge and technology. As Australia both creates intellectual property and is a net importer of innovation, interest lies in balanced protection of intellectual property policy. Meanwhile attention should be paid to the efficiency of domestic IP arrangements (a special regime for SMEs has not proven very effective, for instance).

Expanding access to low-cost, high-speed information and communication technology (ICT)

Widespread access to low cost, high-quality mobile telephony and broadband internet is important for the development and diffusion of many of today's innovations and for narrowing the digital divides within society. As in many other countries, a multiple-operator system has been operating for some time, but nevertheless requires continued attention by regulators to keep up to speed with technological and market developments. Australia faces particular challenges in extending provision to rural and remote areas. While expensive, ensuring good ICT access in these areas, potentially brings wide benefits including improvements in public health, social engagement and education. In fixed-line technology, the wholesaler (National Broadband Network) needs to address concerns that it is not lowering its prices sufficiently quickly as the market develops. In mobile telephony, stronger encouragement of new entrants to retail markets, for instance via policy on the sale of mobile spectrum, would be welcome. Australia currently has only three mobile telephony operators and there is a growing view among international experts that the presence of a fourth operator raises competition significantly (OECD, 2014b). Allowing mobile operators access to the towers being installed for broadband in rural areas would be one practical step to improve choice and make the mobile market more attractive for new entrants.

The regulatory response to disruptors has so far been broadly positive

Echoing global developments, Australia is experiencing a surge in "disruptive" innovations, particularly business-model innovations based on internet platforms. So far the authorities' response has been broadly positive, endeavouring to reshape regulation to accommodate new players while ensuring neutrality of treatment. State-level governments are establishing "cohabitation" arrangements between ride-sharing and taxi services. However, ideally the regulation ought eventually to converge to a common framework both ride-sharing and taxi services. Local governments' regulatory response to new accommodation services via companies such as *Airbnb* has varied widely. As experience deepens with issues such as anti-social behaviour by short-term renters, efforts should be made to identify the most effective regulatory approaches and encourage convergence to them. More generally, barriers to disruption in general framework conditions should be addressed. In particular, competition policy should counter undesirable defence strategies by incumbents. Where tax issues arise from disruption, fair treatment should be sought for incoming enterprises firm and incumbents. The considerations are not always straightforward, as illustrated in the different tax position of those renting out short-term accommodation and hoteliers.

Encouraging productivity and innovation through R&D policy

Strengthening collaboration between business and the research sector

Collaborative research is an important channel for the commercialisation of publicly funded research and knowledge transfer, helping to ensure public returns to support for domestic research. Australia performs poorly on this front (Figure 25). This reflects little priority to collaboration in performance metrics of academics; weak mobility between research and business sectors (including industry placement programmes); and issues in university management of IP. Australia could learn further from international examples of research hubs, such as the Waterloo "triangle" of education, research and innovation in Canada (OECD, 2016a).

Reforms underway, mainly as a part of NISA, attempt to address these issues. A new simplified funding system for university research began operating in early 2017, in which federal block grants for research are determined solely by income from two categories, competitive grants and other sources (including business); these two categories are now given equal weight. One consequence of the reform is that publications will no longer feature in the funding formula (Watt, 2015). The change is intended to increase

Figure 25. **Collaborative research is limited**

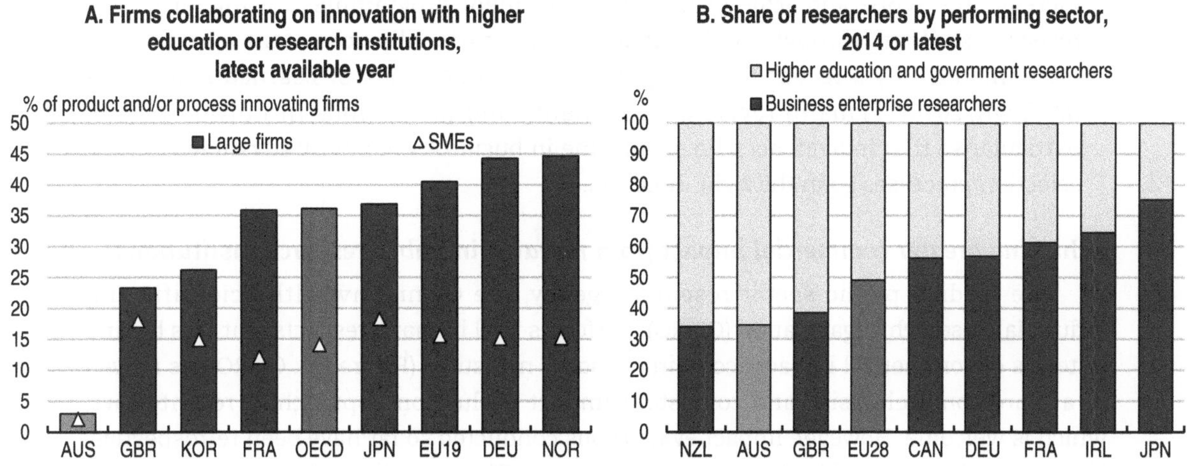

A. Firms collaborating on innovation with higher
education or research institutions,
latest available year

B. Share of researchers by performing sector,
2014 or latest

□ Higher education and government researchers
■ Business enterprise researchers

Source: OECD (2015), OECD Science, Technology and Industry Scoreboard 2015; OECD (2016), Main Science and Technology Indicators: Volume 2015/2.

StatLink http://dx.doi.org/10.1787/888933456865

universities' incentives to collaborate. The reform also aims to make government competitive grants to universities more responsive to applicants' needs. Notably, it moves the Australian Research Council Linkage Projects to a continuous application and assessment process, rather than one round per year, and introduces a fast-track decision-making process (Australian Government, 2015, 2016). Moreover, additional steps are envisaged towards making IP arrangements more effective. These include changes in the funding arrangements for universities from 2017, requiring universities to list their patents generated by publicly funded research on a central information platform (Source IP) and to use simplified contracting arrangements, if requested by collaborative partners.

Regular assessment of funding programmes can help ensure that increased collaboration on research does not come at the expense of quality. The government should also proceed with the development of the new "impact assessment" framework, which facilitates assessment of university research performance in terms of non-academic impact and "engagement" with end-users of research. This will complement the national evaluation framework for the quality of university research. Overall, these reforms go in the right direction in helping create a more collaborative culture between researchers and business and help Australia better translate research knowledge into commercial outcomes. However, there is still scope for improvement, in particular:

● Estimates suggest that only 13% of the firms registered under the *R&D Tax Incentive* (discussed below) are involved in business-focussed collaboration programmes funded by the government (Watt, 2015). Take-up could be increased by implementing simple and flexible governance arrangements, which would reduce unnecessary delays in the negotiation and formalisation of agreements for collaborative research. Greater stability in the menu of programmes and closer monitoring of outcomes would also support higher take-up.

● More effective management of IP created by the universities through the further development and wider use of simplified IP contracts is critical for knowledge exchange and collaboration on the exploitation of IP.

● The mobility between research and business sectors is low (Figure 25). There is room to increase the scope and scale of industry placement programmes for higher degree research students through the introduction of a nationally consistent approach, as recommended by a recent review by the Australian Council of Learned Academies (McGagh, 2016). Plans to revise appointments and promotions in universities, in particular so that individuals who spent time in business are not disadvantaged in the selection processes go in the right direction.

Achieving greater commercial impact from research in public research institutions

The leading public-sector research agency, the Commonwealth Scientific and Industrial Research Organisation (CSIRO), performs well in many respects, but lags behind in terms of commercial impact according to some measures (Figure 26). CSIRO has moved to a more comprehensive and consistent impact evaluation approach in recent years, which is welcome. However, impact evaluations conducted so far have been retrospective. Progress is also required for future impact planning. This is particularly important in view of the larger focus given, compared to the past, on the commercial outcomes under CSIRO's new long-term strategy (CSIRO 2015; The Senate, 2015). It is important that planning and evaluation processes assess the wider impact of commercialisation, including the effect on research excellence and the societal impact.

Figure 26. **Commercial impact could be strengthened**

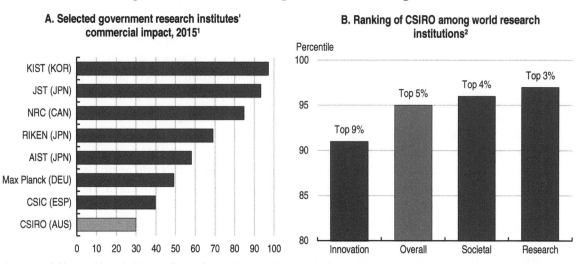

A. Selected government research institutes' commercial impact, 2015[1]

B. Ranking of CSIRO among world research institutions[2]

1. "Commercial impact" is an indicator of how often basic research originating at an Institution has influenced commercial R&D activity, as measured by academic papers cited in patent filings. The selection of institutes is based on comparable annual budget size.
2. "Innovation" measure consists of innovative knowledge (scientific publication output from SCIRO cited in patents) and technological impact (percentage of the scientific publication output cited in patents). "Societal" measure consists of web size and domain's inbound links. "Research" measure consists of output, collaboration, research excellence, leadership and talent pool.

Source: Reuters (2016), Top 25 Global Innovators – Government; Scimago Lab (2016), Scimago Institutions Rankings.

StatLink 🔗 http://dx.doi.org/10.1787/888933456871

A new fund (the *CSIRO Innovation Fund*), announced as part of NISA, was launched at end-2016 by the government to support co-investment in new spin-off and start-up companies created by CSIRO and other research institutions and universities (Australian Government, 2015a). This is a positive initiative in view of the critical role of capital for start-ups. It should also foster greater research-industry collaboration. Investments to be made by the *CSIRO Innovation Fund* however need to favour projects with large commercialisation and productivity-enhancing potential. The government is also transitioning to a common approach for assessing the outcomes and impacts of funded research. This should increase the effectiveness and efficiency of the public-sector research agencies.

Fine-tuning the R&D Tax Incentive

Analysis of the *R&D Tax Incentive* (Incentive) in Chapter 2 of this *Survey* uncovers the challenges in achieving good returns to this form of support. Australia relies heavily on tax incentives, as distinct from grants (Figure 27). Since the introduction of the Incentive in 2011 (which replaced another scheme), participation has increased rapidly, with fiscal costs exceeding forecasts (Australian Government, 2016c). Business R&D intensity data have not so far echoed this development, possibly because of other influences, especially the end of the mining boom. This trend has to be watched, however. The government has initiated a welcome review of the Incentive, with a first assessment (Ferris et al., 2016) circulated for public consultation. This review sensibly proposes fine-tuning the system rather than wholesale change. Areas for improvement include:

- Evidence suggests that only around 10-20% of the total R&D registered under the Incentive is additional (Australian Government, 2016c). Ferris et al. (2016) conclude that the Incentive "falls short of its stated objectives of additionality and spillovers". Measuring and strengthening additionality is difficult and can increase complexity, and compliance and administrative costs. One reform option, suggested by Ferris et al., is the introduction of an intensity threshold (i.e. a minimum amount of R&D expenditure as a proportion of business expenses for eligibility to the Incentive) for recipients of the non-refundable component of the Incentive (larger firms), complemented by an increase in the existing expenditure threshold. Comprehensive analyses are required to assess additionality, as well as the trade-off between increasing additionality and complexity (Appelt et al., 2016).

- The efficiency and effectiveness of the Incentive hinge on careful monitoring of integrity risks and the introduction, if necessary, of tighter, well-targeted compliance measures.

Figure 27. Tax support plays an important role in R&D policy and the cost is rising rapidly

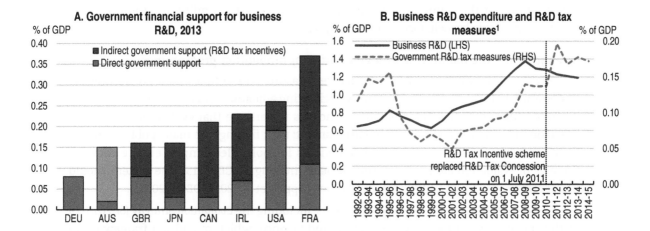

1. 2011-12 was a transitional year in which some firms accessed the R&D Tax Concession while others accessed the R&D Tax Incentive.
Source: Australian Department of Industry, Innovation and Science (2016), The Australian Government's 2016-17 Science, Research and Innovation Budget Tables; OECD (2015), OECD Science, Technology and Industry Scoreboard 2015.

StatLink ᴬᴵˢᴾ *http://dx.doi.org/10.1787/888933456886*

- The Incentive's eligibility criteria are principle-based rather than highly specific. This approach can adapt to changes in the nature of R&D activity, but can also be open to misinterpretation, highlighting the need for clear and consistent interpretation of the eligibility criteria by the authorities. The recent review of the Incentive recommends the development of new guidance (including plain-language summaries and case studies) to increase clarity about the scope of eligible activities and expenses (Ferris et al., 2016).

- The upward risks to the Incentive's costs could be further managed by strengthening provisions for the existing expenditure threshold, so that it also applies to "connected entities", and/or by introducing additional caps (BDO, 2016). For instance, a cap on the refundable tax credit could be considered, while assessing carefully its potential trade-off with additionality.

- Compliance costs could be reduced by adopting a single application process for accessing the R&D tax credit. Currently, companies first register the R&D activities and then make the claim for tax return.

- Industry-research collaboration could be encouraged more, perhaps through an R&D tax premium or by adding criteria relating to collaboration in the current programme.

Improving the governance framework for innovation policy

Australia's science, research and innovation system is complex, with the involvement of several federal government departments and numerous councils, committees and boards. State governments are also involved in policy development and programme design. Federal government investment in research and innovation is spread across 15 portfolios, with their own research and innovation programmes and multiple agencies delivering such programmes (Cutler, 2008). In a welcome step, a new independent board, *Innovation and Science Australia* (ISA), was established in 2016 to provide "strategic, whole-of-government advice on all science, research and innovation matters" (Australian Government, 2015a). ISA could also promote collaboration, as it will be working directly with the industry and community sectors. Its achievements in delivering such outcomes should be closely monitored and evaluated; greater coordination should not come at the expense of the diversity of innovation activities, which would constrain the responsiveness of the innovation system to evolving needs. Some consolidation of the numerous (around 150) small research funding programmes and agreements would also help focus innovation policy.

Strengthening the monitoring and evaluation of innovation programmes

High quality evaluation and performance measurement of innovation programmes is important for efficient and effective policy, facilitating adjustment in the menu of measures towards better outcomes. Good practice principles underscore that evaluations should be based on independent and transparent assessment; their findings are made public; and that they are accompanied by effective mechanisms for policy learning to ensure that the findings of evaluation are guiding future decision-making (OECD, 2015). The system should incorporate both *ex-post* and *ex-ante* evaluations (Appelt et al., 2016; OECD, 2014c).

There have been some welcome initiatives, including the *Evaluation Strategy for 2015-19* of the Department of Industry, Innovation and Science, which provides a framework to guide evaluation and performance measurement (Australian Government, 2015c). The strategy incorporates evaluation across a programme's lifecycle and envisages both prospective and retrospective evaluations. A core goal of the framework is to improve the data available to assess the impacts and outcomes of all programmes.

Table 7. **Past OECD recommendations on framework conditions for business**

Topic and summary of recommendations	Summary of action taken since 2014 *Survey*
Promote competitive markets and cut red tape	
Concentrate on broad support for business: prioritise corporate tax rate cuts, reduce regulatory burdens and tax avoidance	Further corporate tax cuts are underway. The campaign to reduce regulatory burdens continues
Improve infrastructure investment	
Ensure robust and transparent cost-benefit analysis Simplify infrastructure investment processes Improve public-private partnership processes	Infrastructure Australia has been enhanced through online publication of project assessments and new governance arrangements. It has also published a new audit and infrastructure planning documentation and maintenance of an infrastructure priority list New national guidelines on transport assessment and planning have been issued An infrastructure financing unit to develop financing solutions has been announced
Work towards better transport	
Simplify and harmonise road and rail regulation across states Bring in a road-freight pricing scheme Consider reforming arrangements for managing and funding road infrastructure	Reforms of heavy vehicles are underway including consideration of regulation and charging of heavy vehicles and road administration and funding
Improve energy-sector efficiency	
Harmonise interstate regulation Continue privatisation Remove ceilings on retail electricity prices Bring in smart meters	Energy-sector-efficiency reforms are underway, entailing the harmonisation of regulatory frameworks, privatisation; strengthening of competition in retail electricity prices; and, the introduction of demand side initiatives such as the roll out of smart meters

Addressing inequality, enhancing inclusiveness and deepening skills

Innovation policy can play an important role in tackling social issues

Innovation policy in Australia already incorporates considerations of the "wider good" by backing research with potential for significant social return, such as research in many areas of health care and innovations in education. Additional measures could be taken, for instance re-evaluation of innovation support programmes and greater recognition of low-tech or low-cost innovation that bolsters inclusivity. Incorporating innovation-based schemes in the support system for Australia's indigenous communities may yield particularly significant returns, given the very wide socioeconomic gaps with the rest of the population. In addition, ensuring that policy measures regarding broadband and mobile services improve services in areas with indigenous communities in particular would lessen disadvantage arising from digital divides. This would also open more avenues for ICT-based support, for instance in online education and training.

Some progress in welfare policy is being made

As emphasised in previous *Surveys*, the overall architecture of Australia's welfare system is sound. The fiscal demands of the welfare system are comparatively light, which helps keep tax wedges on labour low, supporting employment and competitiveness. The strong emphasis on encouraging transition from welfare to work incentives and activation schemes (run through the Australian Government funded network of private employment service providers) helps limit the number of non-working households dependent on transfers (OECD, 2014a). A renewed emphasis on programmes of support for indigenous job seekers should be a focus to address the gap in employment participation by indigenous and non-indigenous Australians.

Progress is being made on a number of fronts in welfare policy (Table 8). A plan for significant increase in paid parental leave was re-evaluated. Also, as recommended in the previous *Survey*, the government has prioritised child care by announcing a new child care package. In addition, a new programme will offer unemployed youth intensive pre-employment training and short internships (4 to 12 weeks), providing wage subsidies for employers. Moreover, the government will cease the carbon tax compensation for the new recipients of welfare benefits, given the abolition of this tax in 2014, and direct the freed-up resources to the National Disability Insurance Scheme (NDIS). Consideration should be given to also end the compensation for existing welfare recipients. The government will further review over the next 3 years around 90 000 (out of a total more than 800 000) Disability Support Pension (DSP) recipients to assess their capacity to work, with a third of the reviews to include a medical assessment (Australian Government, 2016a). The focus on beneficiaries with a high risk of ineligibility for DSP payments is welcome.

In addition, a new "investment approach" to long-term welfare dependency has begun, illustrating an openness to innovative solutions by the government. Welfare data have been used to identify three groups at risk: young parents, young carers, and young students. Targeted measures will be used to support these groups to transition to employment. Actuarial evaluations will be used to evaluate the effectiveness of interventions and to determine whether an intervention should be scaled up, continued or concluded.

As welfare spending represents a significant share of outlays, particularly at the federal level, it is frequently a target for budgetary measures. While efforts to seek efficiency gains are welcome, the authorities should avoid measures, such as freezes on indexing welfare payouts, so as not to compromise inclusiveness.

General improvement in Australia's education system continues

Education indicators point to an above-average, though not top-ranking, performance. Australian 15 year-olds perform comparatively well in the OECD's PISA tests of reading, mathematics and scientific proficiency and the share of students lacking basic skills is well below that in many other advanced countries (Figure 28). However, performance in PISA tests has declined and differences by socioeconomic background are large (Figure 28). The 2016-17 budget devotes additional funding (of around AUD 1.2 billion between 2018 and 2020) to schools, which is needs-based and contingent on reform to improve student outcomes, including through improving literacy and numeracy, and teaching quality (Australian Government, 2016a). Additional needs-based funding is provided for students with a disability. Early childhood education and training is being boosted through the implementation of in the *Jobs for Families* initiative, which, for instance, is piloting schemes for families where accessing mainstream childcare is not practicable.

In higher education, subsidised student loans (repayment of the loans is income contingent) have been available (since 2009) for courses providing vocational educational and training qualifications; the loans were previously only available for bachelor-level degrees (OECD, 2014a). In principle, this measure has given a welcome boost to vocational education and training, which helps provide skills to innovative sectors. However, in recent years significant problems with the fee system (VET FEE-HELP) have emerged. In particular, inadequate checks on the quality of providers have prompted the emergence of operators selling poor quality courses to students.

Figure 28. **Australia is falling behind leading countries in PISA results**

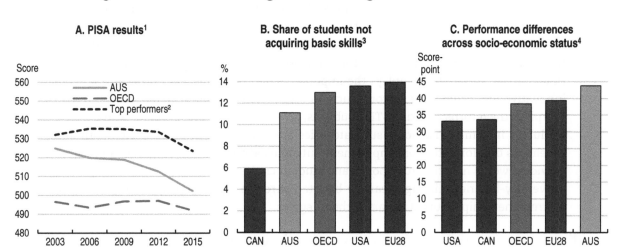

1. Average of reading, mathematics and science. Science scores are available from 2006.
2. Average of Canada, Finland, Japan and Korea.
3. Share of low achievers (below Level 2) in all three subjects (science, reading and mathematics).
4. Score-point difference in science associated with one-unit increase on the PISA index of economic, social and cultural status.
Source: OECD, PISA 2015 Database; OECD (2016), PISA 2015 Results (Volume I): Excellence and Equity in Education.

StatLink ⬛ http://dx.doi.org/10.1787/888933456894

Table 8. **Past OECD recommendations on employment, health and welfare**

Topic and summary of recommendations	Summary of action taken since 2014 *Survey*
Encourage employment	
Improve early childhood education and care (ECEC) to help parents combine work and family life	Additional support for child care has been announced
Improve benefit settings to encourage employment in particular in the disability support system	A new Disability Employment Services model has been designed with implementation intended for 2018
Improve employment services: strengthen funding-performance links, stream claimants more	A new employment services program (*Jobactive*) is operating that aims to help job seekers to find and keep a job
Maintain labour-market flexibility and address supply constraints through migration	
Make negotiation requirements more flexible for new business operations Reform sector-specific labour regulation in negotiated agreements	No major initiative, other than in relation to greenfields agreements for new business operations, where the government has made legislative amendments that provide a new optional six month negotiation timeframe when parties cannot reach agreement
Health care, disability and disadvantage	
In health, increase preventative care, improve services for the elderly and mentally ill, promote primary care Disability support pension. Reduce complexity of the disability system, make it more person-centred	Initiatives in health-care policy include: ● Trialling a programme ('Health Care Homes') that promotes primary care ● Increased dementia research and suicide prevention trials ● More patient choice and consultation for home-care services for the aged ● Ongoing implementation of disability care and services (the National Disability Insurance Scheme (NDIS)
Welfare	
Better target superannuation (pension) tax concessions Improve services for those with multiple disadvantages	Legislation to implement a suite of reforms to better target the superannuation tax concessions, and improve the flexibility and integrity of the superannuation system has passed parliament

Similar to other OECD countries, Australia's education policy favours science, technology, engineering and maths (STEM) skills on the basis that these are key for productive and innovative sectors. NISA continues this approach with programmes to increase primary and secondary students' interest in ICT, to promote STEM skills (for instance by expanding prizes for science) and to encourage women in science. However this approach downplays the importance of other subjects in providing skills in innovative and productive sectors, such as innovation-related arts disciplines. It also overplays the returns to taking STEM subjects, given the career prospects for tertiary-level graduates in some STEM some sub-categories are not strong. Improving the depth and timeliness of information on employment outcomes across different subjects and across providers would help fine-tune policy and student choices. Innovation-relevant skills and university-business linkages can be boosted through encouraging students to take "entrepreneurship" courses as part of their degrees.

Tackling environmental challenges: progress in greenhouse-gas emission policy

Australia's carbon intensity of production is around one-third greater than the OECD average, and per capita emissions are 50% higher – though in other respects air quality is generally good (Figure 29). These high emissions relate more to the energy mix than to energy intensity, which is somewhat above the OECD average but improving. Renewables, currently mostly from hydroelectric generation, have picked up but still account for only a small share of energy production compared with the OECD average. Australia's new greenhouse-gas (GHG) reduction target, in accordance with the Paris Agreement 2015, includes reducing GHG emissions by 26-28% below 2005 levels by 2030, which according to official estimates translates to an emission level of about 440 million tonnes of CO_2-equivalent (CO_2-eq) by 2030 (Australian Government, 2015d; Figure 30).

Greenhouse-gas reduction centres on the Direct Action Plan, which was initiated in 2014 following the repeal of the Emissions Trading Scheme, a carbon-credit and purchase system. Under the centrepiece Emissions Reduction Fund, emitters receive payment for emission reductions, rather than paying to emit. Using a reverse auction, the authorities select emission-reduction projects from a pool of proposals submitted by emitters (such as energy producers). The authorities then contract with emitters to buy the selected projects' emission reductions on delivery. The three auctions conducted up to April 2016 have resulted in a commitment to purchase a total of 143 million tonnes CO_2-eq with a value of AUD 1.7 billion, implying an average emission-reduction cost of AUD 11.9 per tonne. The government aims for a total commitment of AUD 2.6 billion, which, if the same average price results from the remaining auctions, will represent a commitment to purchase about 210 million tonnes CO_2-eq.

The Emission Reduction Fund, in principle, can achieve the same emission-reduction outcomes as alternative economic mechanisms, such as a carbon tax or a cap-and-trade system. However, it entails fiscal expense rather than increased revenue. Also, as the Fund focuses on specific emission-reduction projects, rather than total emissions, it does not strongly guarantee achievement of Australia's commitments. To tackle this, a "safeguard mechanism" has been operating since July 2016, as supported by the 2014 Survey (Table 9). The mechanism discourages large industrial facilities from exceeding a historical emission baseline, to counter the risk that emission reductions paid for under the Emission Reduction Fund are "undone" by emissions elsewhere. Should emitters exceed baseline

Figure 29. **Green growth indicators for Australia**

A. CO₂ intensity

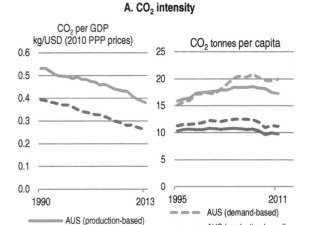

B. Energy intensity

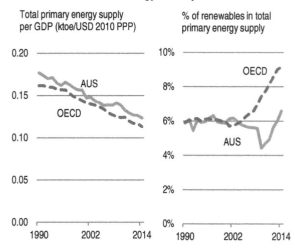

C. Population exposure to air polution

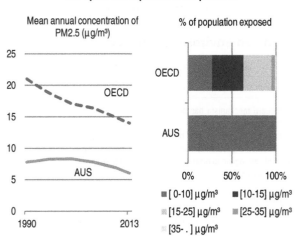

D. Waste generation and recycling

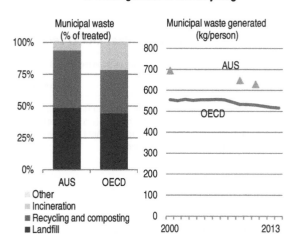

E. Green taxation

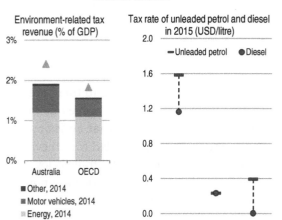

F. Environmentally-related inventions

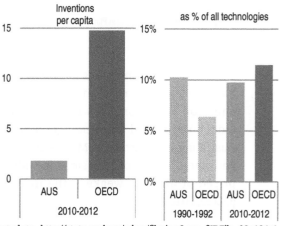

Source: OECD (2016) Green Growth Indicators (database). For detailed metadata, *http://stats.oecd.org/wbos/fileview2.aspx?IDFile=02a134e1-c3ec-4c5c-9a05-4ebb41a60539.*

StatLink ᴴᵀᵀᴾ *http://dx.doi.org/10.1787/888933456908*

Figure 30. **Australia's greenhouse-gas emission reduction is now focused on the target for 2030**

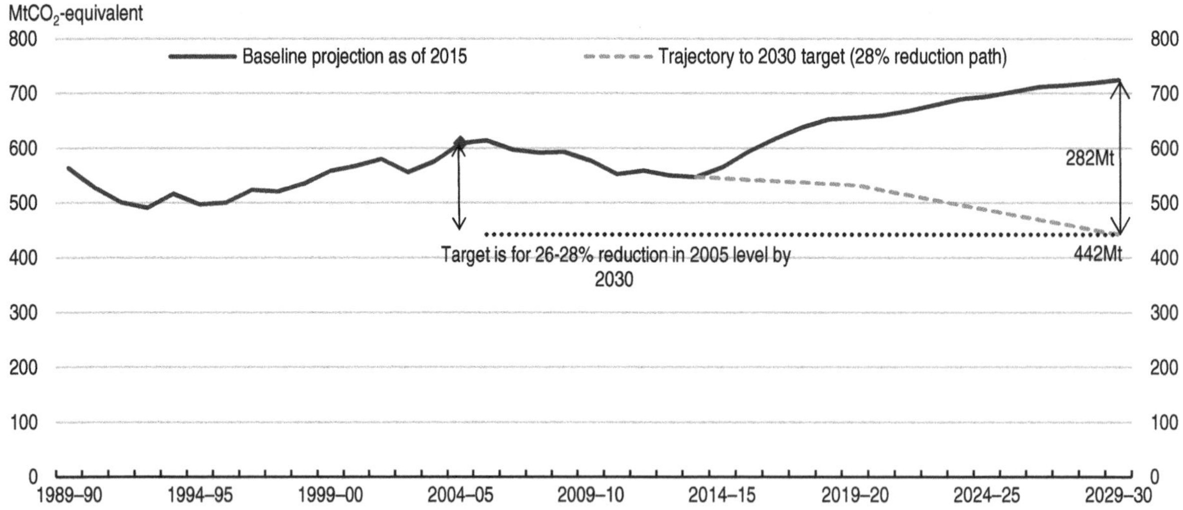

MtCO$_2$-equivalent

Source: Australian Department of the Environment (2015), Australia's emissions projections 2014-15; Energetics (2016), Modelling and analysis of Australia's abatement opportunities; OECD, Greenhouse gas emissions (database).

StatLink ⬛ http://dx.doi.org/10.1787/888933456919

Table 9. **Past OECD recommendations on environment policy**

Topic and summary of recommendations	Summary of action taken since 2014 *Survey*
Achieve greenhouse-gas emission targets:	
Ensure the proposed Emission Reduction Fund is efficient through: i) robust measurement and verification methods; and ii) implementation of a safeguard mechanism that prevents offsetting emissions elsewhere in the economy	A safeguard mechanism has been operation since July 2016. Key features include: • Net emission baselines have been set for about 140 large emitters based on the highest emissions from 2009-10 to 2013-14 • A facility struggling to meet its baseline can purchase carbon credits from other facilities
Make transport policy greener	
Enact the proposal to index excise duty on retail fuel, expand other use-based vehicle charges and extend public transport	Indexing of the fuel excise tax to the Consumer Price Index was reintroduced in November 2014 Plans to reform road-user charging, initially for heavy vehicles, are progressing
Continue strong commitment to water reform	
Complete the Murray-Darling Basin Plan	The seven-year implementation phase (which began in 2012) continues

emissions, they can purchase carbon credits from other facilities. The safeguard therefore has an element of a cap-and-trade system and in future it could play a more active role in emission reduction. This may prove an attractive option in the event that emission reductions beyond those brought about by the Direct Action Plan are needed to achieve Australia's commitments. More generally the price of carbon emissions in Australia is low, with large shares of emissions in industry, electricity, agriculture and fisheries are not priced at all. This weakens the incentives to cut carbon in a cost-effective manner (OECD, 2016b).

Changes are underway to reduce grant-based support and increase equity and debt support for green innovation. These involve a new fund, the Clean Energy Innovation Fund, which will make loans or take equity stakes in companies engaged in commercialising emerging technologies. The authorities envisage that this fund will take over much of the role currently played by the Australian Renewable Energy Agency, which provides grants to companies. The Clean Energy Finance Corporation which provides loans for the installation of established clean-energy technologies will continue with its current role. The shift away from grants towards loan and equity support means more fiscal "return" to support but might mean there is less early stage support.

Road-based transport is dominant in Australia and so incorporating environmental considerations in regulation and taxation that relate to vehicle use is particularly important. Inflation indexing on retail-fuel excise has been re-introduced, a welcome move that will end erosion of the real value of fuel taxation and help boost the level of environmental taxation (Figure 29). Room for further improvement in fuel taxation remains. Currently, Australia charges the same excise per litre on diesel and gasoline, which is a superior approach to that of those countries where excise on diesel is less than that on gasoline. However, as argued in an OECD working paper (Harding, 2014), in light of diesel's additional disadvantages, notably in terms of local air pollution, the optimal excise on diesel ought to be above that for petroleum. As underscored in the 2014 *Survey*, charges for car use rather than car ownership should be the central pillar of policy, and would provide further justification to reform the various state-level taxes relating to car ownership. In a welcome development, the authorities are pressing on with plans to reform road-user charges, beginning with heavy trucks.

Water resources (the subject of in-depth review in the 2008 *Survey*) are a key constraint for agriculture. Drought conditions have, in the past, threatened the supply of water to Sydney, which now has a wind-powered desalination plant as reserve supply (WaterNSW, 2016). Groundwater depletion and salinity are problems in the Murray-Darling basin, the principal river system, but since basin management techniques have been introduced groundwater levels have recovered in some areas since the 1990s (Smerdon et al., 2012).

Bibliography

APRA (Australian Prudential Regulation Authority) (2014), "APRA outlines further steps to reinforce sound residential mortgage lending practices", *Media Release*, December 9th, 2014.

APRA (2016), APRA Insight, Issue Two, 2016, Australian Prudential Regulation Authority, Canberra.

Appelt S., et al. (2016), "R&D Tax Incentives: Evidence on Design, Incidence and Impacts", *OECD Science, Technology and Industry Policy Papers*, No. 31.

Australian Government (2014), Financial System Inquiry, Final Report, Commonwealth of Australia, 2014.

Australian Government (2015a), *National Innovation & Research Agenda*, Commonwealth of Australia, Canberra.

Australian Government (2015b), Competition Policy Review, Final Report, March 2015, Canberra.

Australian Government (2015c), *Evaluation Strategy 2015-19*, Commonwealth of Australia.

Australian Government (2015d), Australia's 2030 Climate Change Target, Commonwealth of Australia, 2015.

Australian Government (2016a), Budget 2016-17 Budget Strategy and Outlook, Budget Paper No. 1, Commonwealth of Australia, 2016.

Australian Government (2016b), "Delivering a High-Performing Research Sector in Australia: Watt Review Response", May.

Australian Government (2016c), "R&D Tax Incentive Review Issues Paper", February.

BDO (2016), "R&D Tax Incentive Review – Issues Paper Response", February.

CSIRO (2015), *Australia's Innovation Catalyst: CISIRO Strategy 2020*, July Canberra.

Cutler, T. (2008), *Venturous Australia: Building Strength in Innovation*, Melbourne.

Fall and Fournier (2015), Macroeconomic uncertainties, prudent debt targets and fiscal rules, OECD Economics Department Working Papers, No. 1230.

Ferris B., Finkel A. and J. Fraser (2016), *Review of the R&D Tax Incentive*, April.

Harding, M. (2014), The Diesel Differential, Differences in the Tax Treatment of Gasoline and Diesel for Road Use, OECD Taxation Working Papers, No. 21.

Hermansen, M. and O. Röhn (2015), "Economic Resilience: he Usefulness of Early Warning Indicators in OECD Countries", OECD Economics Department Working Paper, No. 1250.

McGagh, J. et al. (2016), Review of Australia's Research Training System, Report for the Australian Council of Learned Academies (ACOLA).

OECD (2014a), OECD *Economic Surveys, Australia*, OECD Publishing, Paris.

OECD (2014b), "Wireless Market Structures and Network Sharing", *OECD Digital Economy Papers*, No. 243.

OECD (2014c), *OECD Science, Technology and Industry Outlook 2014*, OECD Publishing.

OECD (2015), *The Innovation Imperative: Contributing to Productivity, Growth, and Well-Being*, OECD Publishing, Paris.

OECD (2016a), "Enhancing the Contributions of Higher Educaction and Research Institutions to Innovation", Background Document, OECD High Level Event on the Knowledge Triangle, Paris September 2016.

OECD (2016b), *Pricing CO2 Through Taxes and Emission Trading Systems*, OECD Publishing.

Productivity Commission (2016), *Overcoming Indigenous Disadvantage: key indicators 2016*, Commonwealth of Australia, 2016.

Röhn, O., A. Caldera Sánchez, M. Hermansen and M. Rasmussen (2015), "Economic Resilience: A New Set of Vulnerability Indicators for OECD Countries", OECD Economics Department Working Paper, No. 1249.

Smerdon B., F. Marsto. and T. Ransley (2012), "Water resource assessment for the Great Artesian Basin: Synthesis of a report to the Australian Government from the CSIRO Great Artesian Basin Water Resource Assessment".

The Senate (2015), Australia's Innovation System, Economic References Committee, December.

Water NSW, (2015), "Water Security Projects: Recommission and upgrade of the current desalination facility in Broken Hill".

Watt, I., (2015), *Review of the Research Policy and Funding Arrangements*, Report, November.

ANNEX

Follow-up to previous OECD policy recommendations

This annex reviews action taken on recommendations from previous Surveys. They cover macroeconomic and structural policy priorities. Each recommendation is followed by a note of actions taken since the December 2014 Survey. Recommendations that are new in this Survey are listed in the relevant chapter.

Monetary and financial stability

Topic and summary of recommendations	Summary of action taken since 2014 Survey
Improve the functioning of the housing market	
Continue intensive monitoring of the housing market; maintain deep micro-prudential oversight and consider using macro-prudential tools to bolster credit safeguards and signal concern	Use of macro-prudential measures has begun (alongside continued deep micro-prudential oversight). These, inter alia, put banks under pressure to: ● limit investor lending to 10% growth annually ● ramp up assessment of potential borrowers ability afford mortgage repayments ● cease a variety of high-risk lending practices
Facilitate housing supply in particular through planning regulation reform at state and territory level	State-level planning regulation reform continues
Examine competition and credit issues in the financial sector	
Reduce banking sector privileges. Consider: reducing banks' implicit guarantees, tackling risk-weighting advantages in mortgage lending, improving credit databases	Risk weightings on mortgage lending were raised in July 2015 for banks that use the internal ratings-based models

Maintaining fiscal prudence and ensuring efficient tax and public spending

Topic and summary of recommendations	Summary of action taken since 2014 *Survey*
Strengthen mechanism that aid fiscal discipline	
Prioritise medium-term fiscal consolidation to rebuild fiscal buffers in light of Australia's exposure to external risk. Consider establishing a stabilisation fund	Federal-budget consolidation remains ambitious, deficit outcomes have fallen short of goals. No progress has been made in widening the use of stabilisation funds
Tax reform	
Rebalance the tax mix; shift away from income and transaction taxes Make greater use of efficient tax bases such as the Goods and Services Tax and land tax	Tax measures in the 2016-17 budget include further reduction in the rate of corporate tax and further measures to combat base erosion and profit shifting in corporate taxation. The Government has added GST to the online purchase of digital products and service and is introducing legislation to add GST to low-value imported goods. As regard making greater use of land tax (and less use of inefficient taxes), so far only one jurisdiction, Australian Capital Territory, has embarked on a major reform. The reform is increasing land taxes, reducing transfer duties on conveyances and abolishing insurance taxes. As regards other jurisdictions, New South Wales, for instance has increased land taxes to cover the emergency services levy (which used to be part of insurance taxes) and South Australia is abolishing stamp duties on commercial properties, but not, so far, planning to increase reliance on land taxes.
Improving the federal-state system	
Reform State financing: reduce grant conditionality further, instigate State-level tax reforms to enhance funding autonomy Address federal-State responsibilities: improve coordination and co-operation and in some cases, health care in particular, consider a reallocation of responsibilities	No major initiative

Framework conditions for business

Topic and summary of recommendations	Summary of action taken since 2014 *Survey*
Promote competitive markets and cut red tape	
Concentrate on broad support for business; prioritise corporate-tax rate cuts, reduce regulatory burdens and tax avoidance	Further corporate tax cuts are underway. Campaigns to reduce regulatory burdens by AUS 1 billion each year continue.
Improve infrastructure investment	
Ensure robust and transparent cost-benefit analysis Simplify infrastructure investment processes Improve public-private partnership processes	Infrastructure Australia's (IA) has been enhanced through a number of measures, including: • all projects assessed by IA are now published online; • new governance arrangements for IA are in place; • IA has released the Australian Infrastructure Audit (2015) and the Australian Infrastructure Plan (2016); and • IA is maintaining an Infrastructure Priority List. In August 2016, the federal government, in consultation with state and territory governments, released its revised national guide to transport assessment and planning. These guidelines provide a comprehensive and consistent framework for developing transport systems across Australian governments. In April 2016, the government announced, that it would establish an infrastructure financing unit (IFU) to develop financing solutions to deliver key government projects.
Work towards better transport	
Simplify and harmonise road and rail regulation across states Bring in a road-freight pricing scheme Consider reforming arrangements for managing and funding road infrastructure.	Comprehensive reforms of heavy vehicles are underway, including the consideration of alternative charging arrangements. The reform process includes considering more efficient organisational, regulatory and governance arrangements for administering and funding roads. An initial analysis of the high level costs and benefits of extending reform to light vehicles is also being undertaken
Improve energy-sector efficiency	
Harmonise interstate regulation Continue privatisation Remove ceilings on retail electricity prices Bring in smart meters	Reforms are being pursued across jurisdictions to improve energy sector efficiency. These include the harmonisation of regulatory frameworks; ongoing efforts to privatise network businesses; improvements to competition of retail electricity prices; and the introduction of demand side initiatives such as the roll out of smart meters. The Council of Australian Governments Energy Council continues to monitor progress and drive economic reforms

Employment, health and welfare

Topic and summary of recommendations	Summary of action taken since 2014 *Survey*
Encourage employment	
Improve early childhood education and care (ECEC) to help parents combine work and family life	Additional support for child care has been announced
Improve benefit settings to encourage employment in particular in the disability support system	The Government has announced that it will reform its Disability Employment Framework. The Government is currently finalising the design of its new Disability Employment Services model and intends to undertake further consultation ahead of the planned introduction of the new framework in 2018.
Improve employment services: strengthen funding-performance links, stream claimants more	The Government introduced a new employment services program *jobactive* in 2015. The new *jobactive* programme is designed to help more job seekers to find and keep a job and move from welfare to work.

Maintain labour-market flexibility and address supply constraints through migration	
Make negotiation requirements more flexible for new business operations Reform sector-specific labour regulation in negotiated agreements	No major initiative , other than in relation to greenfields agreements for new business operations, where the government has made legislative amendments that provide a new optional six month negotiation timeframe when parties cannot reach agreement

Health care, disability and disadvantage	
In health increase preventative care, improve services for the elderly and mentally ill, promote primary care Disability support pension. Reduce complexity of the disability system, make it more person-centred	A number of programs have been initiated in the area discussed. Some include: • Primary care: Trialling Health Care Homes to promote primary care, deal with Chronic conditions and prevent escalation of health risks • Mental Health: dementia research and Headspace funding, suicide prevention trials • Aged Care: Consumer Directed Care extended to all Home Care Packages so that consumers have greater choice in the services received. • Disability Care: Implementing the National Disability Insurance Scheme (NDIS) to provide people-centred care by giving choices on how persons with a disability utilise services

Welfare	
Better target superannuation (pension) tax concessions Improve services for those with multiple disadvantages	Legislation to implement a suite of reforms to better target the superannuation tax concessions, and improve the flexibility and integrity of the superannuation system has passed parliament

Environment policy

Topic and summary of recommendations	Summary of action taken since 2014 *Survey*
Achieve greenhouse-gas emission targets:	
Ensure the proposed Emission Reduction Fund is efficient through: i) robust measurement and verification methods; and ii) implementation of a safeguard mechanism that prevents offsetting emissions elsewhere in the economy	A safeguard mechanism has been operation since July 2016: key features: • Net emission baselines have been set for about 140 large emitters based on the highest emissions in the five years 2009-10 to 2013-14 • A facility struggling to meet its baseline can purchase carbon credits from other facilities
Make transport policy greener	
Enact the proposal to index excise duty on retail fuel, expand other use-based vehicle charges and extend public transport	Indexing of the fuel excise tax to the Consumer Price Index was reintroduced in November 2014
Continue strong commitment to water reform	
Complete the Murray-Darling Basin Plan	The Murray-Darling Basin Plan was introduced in November 2012 with a seven year implementation phase. The core function of the Basin Plan is to set long term limits on water extraction from river valleys and groundwater within the Basin. These sustainable diversion limits will commence in 2019 through state government water resource plans.

Thematic chapters

Chapter 1

Creating good conditions for innovation-driven productivity gains

Innovation is key to boosting Australia's productivity and inclusiveness. This chapter examines the policies that create good conditions for innovation, not only in science and technology but also wider forms, such as business-model innovation. Competition and flexible markets are particularly important in the Australian context. Also there is room to improve the environment for firm entry and exit, and intellectual property arrangements. However, the returns to public spending on Australia's numerous innovation-related SME support schemes are uncertain. Federal and state governments are taking a positive approach to the new wave of "disruptive" service-sector innovations, such as those underway in personal transport, accommodation, legal and financial services. Harnessing the full benefits of today's innovation requires household and business have access to high-speed ICT; and there is room for improvement on this front in Australia. In education, Australia's STEM-oriented strategy could be strengthened. Innovation in public-services should receive considerable attention as this can raise aggregate productivity and improve living standards.

The statistical data for Israel are supplied by and under the responsibility of the relevant Israeli authorities. The use of such data by the OECD is without prejudice to the status of the Golan Heights, East Jerusalem and Israeli settlements in the West Bank under the terms of international law.

Innovation is a key driver of productivity and sustainable growth in advanced countries and is therefore a central theme of economic policy. In Australia a new policy campaign – *the National Innovation and Science Agenda (NISA)* - is adding fresh impetus to reform. This chapter focuses on the "framework" policies that influence Australia's capacity for productivity growth through innovation. These include policies that not only influence the science-technology segment of the innovation spectrum, but also the innovation embodied in "sharing economy" business models and innovation in public-sector services. Australia's targeted innovation policy instruments, which are chiefly aimed at boosting R&D activity, are considered in Chapter 2 of this *Survey*.

Gauging Australia's productivity performance and innovation capacity

A familiar picture of weak productivity growth in recent years

Echoing developments in many other economies, Australia's productivity growth has been comparatively weak in recent years (Figure 1.1). This is the case for both trend labour productivity (which reflects the deepening of physical and human capital as well as innovation processes) and total-factor productivity (TFP, which more closely reflects innovation). A downward trend began in the late 1990s, with an extended pause during the peak of the mining boom. Various factors, over and above capital deepening and innovation, have been influencing Australia's productivity, ranging from the fading effects of past economic reforms to growth in investments whose returns are not fully captured in measured output (Box 1.1). Nevertheless, as other economies have been experiencing

Figure 1.1. **Australia has joined the productivity slowdown**

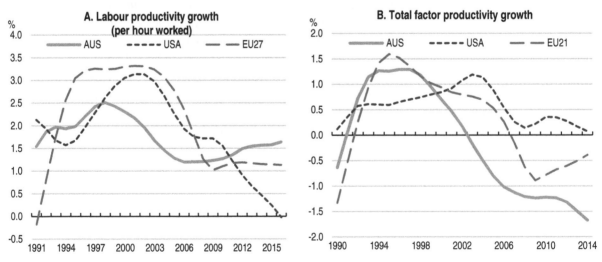

Note: Data are based on total GDP and smoothed by the Hodrick-Prescott filter. EU data refer to unweighted average of those with suitable data availability.

Source: The Conference Board (2016), The Conference Board Total Economy Database.

StatLink ⟨⟩ *http://dx.doi.org/10.1787/888933456928*

Box 1.1. **Influences on productivity trends in Australia**

There have been a number of influences on Australian productivity in recent decades, over and above innovation-related processes. Commonly cited are:

- **Fading positive impacts of 1990s microeconomic reform.** It is widely believed that Australian productivity benefited substantially from microeconomic reforms of the early 1990s (see, for instance, Banks, 2010) and that the productivity slowdown is partly due to the fading of these effects.

- **Long time scales in building resource-sector facilities**. In resource sectors it often takes considerable time to construct new facilities. During the construction phase there is investment (but with no corresponding boost to output), dampening productivity growth. Once facilities are completed and production begins there is then a boost to productivity. This "investment cycle" influence on productivity has been important in recent years due to heavy investment in certain sectors, such as liquefied natural gas production.

- **Utility-sector investment.** Australia's utilities sectors have embarked on substantial investment – invariably in network infrastructure (e.g. poles and wires in electricity transmission). Such investment does not always translate into more output per se (e.g. more electricity generated), but brings improvements in other dimensions (e.g. reliability of electricity supply) that are not captured in gross-domestic product.

- **Increasing regulation and legislation related to concerns about risk**. Some (for example Eslake, 2011), argue that attention to certain risks in recent years (notably financial-sector risk and security risk) has prompted a wave of regulation and legislation. This can mandate investment for which there is no apparent return in GDP data (but which may nevertheless perhaps bring positive benefits, such as reduced risk of terrorist attacks or financial-sector meltdown). Furthermore, such regulation and legislation can limit productivity enhancing innovation (for instance by discouraging high-risk financing).

- **Reluctance to invest by business since the global-financial crisis (GFC)**. Similar to elsewhere, post-GFG business investment has been lacklustre. Indeed, the nominal value of annual non-mining investment has remained more or less unchanged since the crisis. A prolonged phase of weak business investment growth does not auger well for innovation-driven productivity as it implies a slowdown in the pace adoption of new technologies (the "embodied technical change" in new machinery and equipment).

similar trend decline, these factors are unlikely to fully explain the Australian trend; a downturn in productivity gains from innovation is almost certainly underway.

Future global trends in innovation and technology and their implications for productivity will be as relevant to Australia as they are to other economies. Unsurprisingly, views are wide-ranging. Proceedings from a conference on productivity and innovation (OECD, 2014a) illustrate that some believe productivity gains on the scale of those from past core innovations (such as electrification and the internal combustion engine) are unlikely. Others, in contrast, expect acceleration in technological change in the coming decades. The divergent views underscore the uncertainty of future technological development and the importance of factoring this into innovation-policy strategy. Most importantly, uncertainty implies giving weight to improving general framework conditions for innovation and to exercising caution in targeted policies that are pitched at particular sectors or technologies.

Investment in innovation is well below top-ranking countries

A key concept for assessing innovative activity is Knowledge-Based Capital (KBC). Measures of KBC indicate the depth of economies' engagement in innovation-related activities. The OECD's KBC measure includes valuations of innovative property (such as R&D), computerised information, and economic competencies (such as organisational capital, branding, worker training). The KBC approach allows innovation to be integrated into a production-function framework, with "investment" in this form of capital being analogous to that in physical and human capital.

Australia's investment in KBC is considerably lower than that of several innovation-intensive countries (Figure 1.2). This partly reflects middle-ranking R&D spending, which is discussed in detail in Chapter 2 of this report. In addition, Australia ranks poorly in the "software and databases" and the "brand equity, firm-specific human capital, organisation capital" components of the KBC data. Low or middle-ranking scores in such indicators provide pointers to policy issues. However, some caution is required in interpretation. There can be sound reasons for cross-country differences in R&D spending. For example, some economies are more specialised in R&D intensive sectors (such as pharmaceuticals) than others. The same applies for the other forms of KBC. The key question is whether policy support is enabling an appropriate level of innovation given the structure and context of the economy. The complications of the linkages between R&D and productivity are illustrated in Australian data, for instance see Box 1.2.

Figure 1.2. **Investment in knowledge-based capital (KBC) is comparatively low**

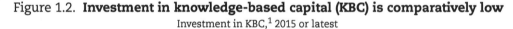

Investment in KBC,[1] 2015 or latest

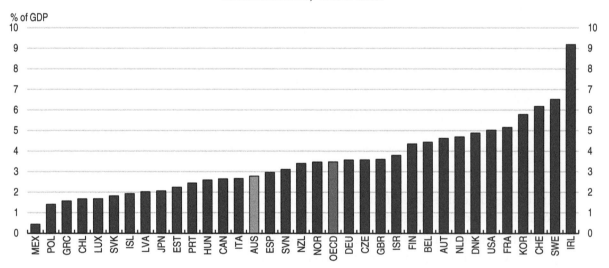

1. Includes R&D, mineral exploration and evaluation, computer software and databases, entertainment, literary and artistic originals, and other IPPs.
Source: OECD (2017), OECD National Accounts (database).

StatLink ⬛⬛ *http://dx.doi.org/10.1787/888933456936*

Box 1.2. **Links between R&D and productivity in Australian data**

Many studies have found supporting evidence for a link between R&D investment and productivity (for example, Egert, 2016; Khan et al., 2010; Guellec and van Pottelsberghe de la Potterie, 2003). A central theme of many of these studies is that productivity can be driven by R&D investment from several sources: domestic business research, public research, but also R&D in other countries. For this *Survey* an econometric exercise was carried out with time-series data for three Australian industry sectors (agriculture, mining and manufacturing covering 1990 to 2014). Business, foreign and public R&D stocks were used separately as regressors to explain sectoral labour productivity. Control variables included labour quality, capital intensity, trade openness, business cycle and market regulations.

Results for two specifications that showed among the most statistically robust connections between R&D and productivity are shown below. As a priori reasoning suggests, domestic business R&D has the largest coefficient and is the most significant statistically. Foreign R&D indeed has an impact too. The apparent absence of any significant impact of public R&D stocks on productivity probably reflects that this exercise cannot capture the more complicated connections between public R&D and productivity.

Various uncertainties and challenges in measuring the magnitude of the effects of R&D on productivity emerged in the exercise. The regression variants that were conducted illustrated a sensitivity of the results to specification. This was also found in previous research. Around a decade ago Australia's Productivity Commission conducted an exercise that examined a very large number of models and combinations of explanatory variables (Shanks and Zheng, 2006). Key issues arise in measurement especially, of R&D capital (i.e. knowledge stocks) and productivity, the role of macroeconomic "shocks" and choice of control variables.

Estimation results

Labour productivity as the dependent variable[1]	Explanatory variables			Control variables	
	Business R&D stocks per VA (t-1)[1]	Foreign R&D stocks per VA (t-2)[1]	Public R&D stocks per VA (t-2)[1]	Capital intensity	Other control variables
Fixed-effect regression with AR(1) disturbance	0.281***	0.252*	0.0723	0.0206***	Trade openness, Market regulations, Time-fixed effect
Pooled OLS	1.137***	0.706***	-0.105	0.0210***	

* p-value < 0.10; ** p < 0.05; *** p < 0.01.
1. In logarithmic scale.
Source: OECD calculations.

Enhancing productivity should be a core objective of innovation policy

For many advanced economies there is comparatively little room for productivity gains through "plain vanilla" capital deepening (i.e. productivity growth from greater use of machinery, equipment and buildings in production processes). Instead, TFP growth becomes the main vehicle for productivity advances and therefore innovation-related processes are key. In Australia's case, as a small, capital importing country, capital deepening has historically been the main driver of labour productivity growth. Improving TFP growth will also be important to boost productivity growth even further. By consequence, raising productivity needs to be a central strand of innovation policy, alongside the achievement of non-economic goals, such as improving health outcomes and tackling climate and other environmental issues.

There are many routes through which innovation can boost productivity. Figure 1.3 presents a schematic picture of the Australian context:

- **Most productivity-enhancing innovation in Australia draws on the "outside".** With the internationalisation of research and production, most productivity-enhancing innovation comes from the outside Australia through either tangible new products, machinery and equipment, or intangibles, such as software or innovation in processes. "Imported" innovation's growing role is illustrated in the growing gap between the charges and fees paid for foreign intellectual property (IP) and those received for Australian IP (Figure 1.4). Also, the increasing internationalisation of production ("global value chains") means the diffusion of innovation via supply chains is becoming more important. Recent OECD research (Saia et al., 2015) finds that diffusion via global value chains and business R&D is weak in Australia while that via skill allocation and managerial quality is middle ranking (Figure 1.5).

- **Domestic research contributes to productivity in complex ways.** Research carried out by Australian universities and research institutes most directly impacts domestic productivity when these institutions work with the business sector (for example through commissioned research or collaborative research). In addition, university and research-institute research contributions to global knowhow feed indirectly through to domestic innovation-driven productivity improvement. There is evidence of other linkages. In particular, basic research activity boosts productivity, one channel being through positive effects on the effectiveness of applied research (OECD, 2015a; Saia et al., 2015). Also, as government has considerable steerage on the domestic research sector, for instance through federal transfers for research to universities, this sector is a core focus of targeted R&D policy (see Chapter 2 of this *Survey*).

Figure 1.3. **Influences on business-sector innovation and productivity**

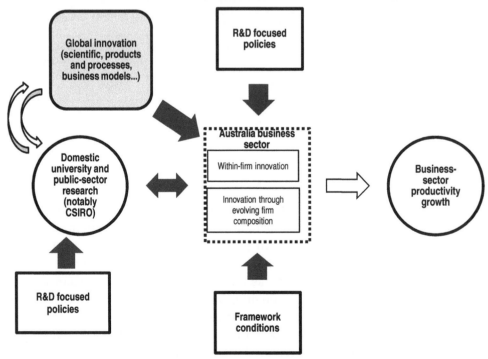

Source: OECD.

Figure 1.4. **Spending on imported intellectual property has become increasingly important**

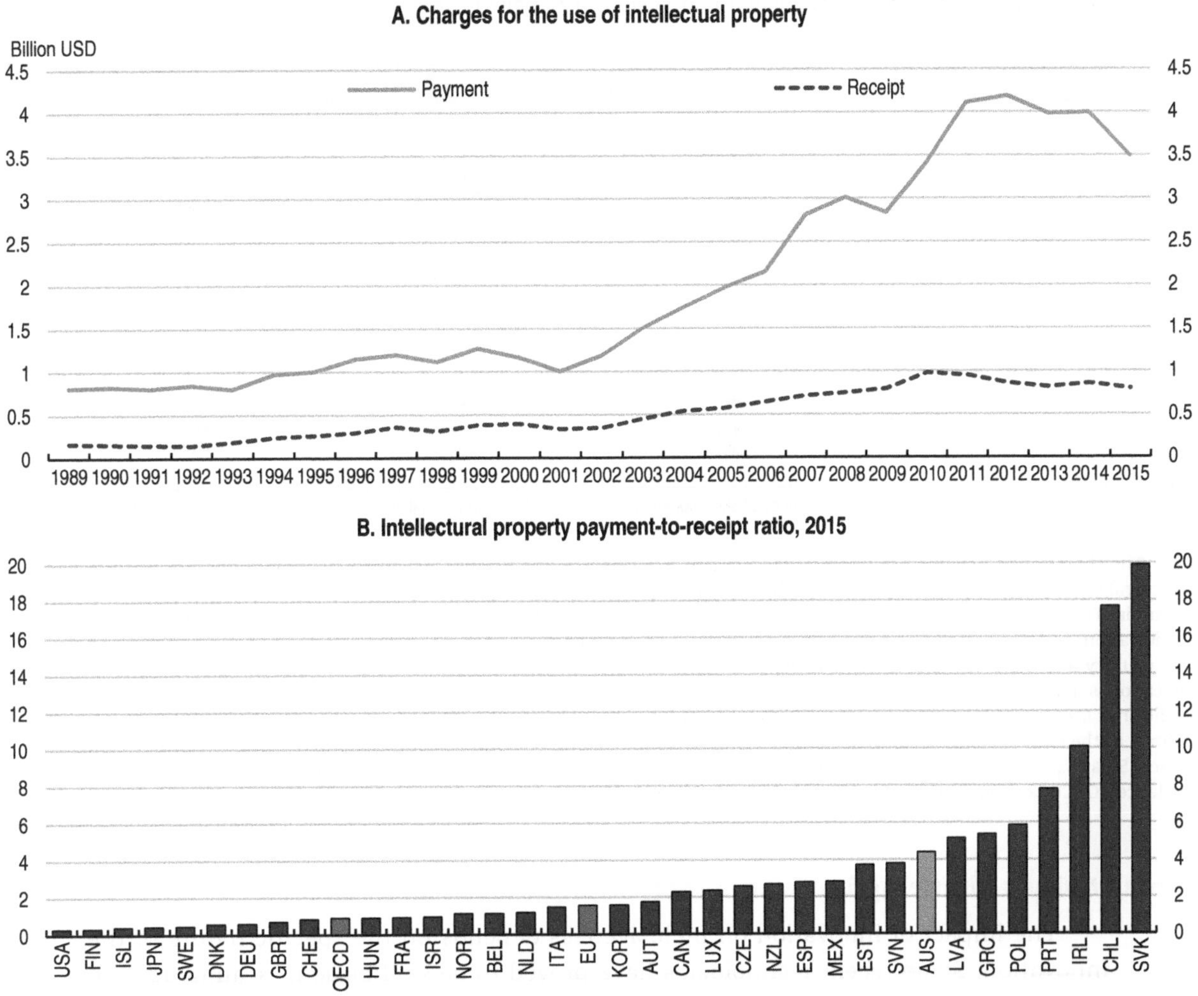

A. Charges for the use of intellectual property

B. Intellectual property payment-to-receipt ratio, 2015

Source: World Bank (2016), World Development Indicators database.

StatLink *http://dx.doi.org/10.1787/888933456949*

- **Reallocation mechanisms matter for innovation,** because they influence how many firms are innovative and operating at technological frontiers. Innovation policy typically focuses on within-firm innovation, however reallocation effects are also important. Of particular relevance are the notions of "creative destruction" (new technologies replacing old ones through the entry, exit, expansion and contraction of firms) and distinctions between firms at the technological frontier and those behind the curve ("lagging" firms). Issues in reallocation are thought to explain much of the lacklustre productivity performance of OECD economies in recent years. According to recent firm-level evidence (OECD, 2016), firms at the technological frontier are delivering productivity gains but "lagging" firms are not keeping up as before; diffusion is seemingly stalling.

Figure 1.5. **Structural factors and learning from the global frontier**

Estimated frontier spillover (% per annum) associated with 2% point increase in MFP growth at the global frontier

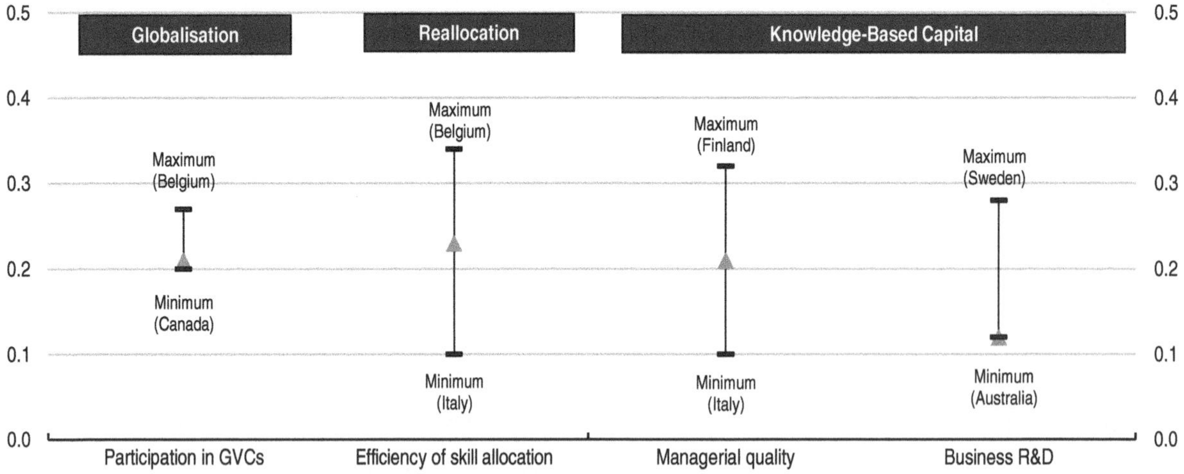

Note: The chart shows how the sensitivity of MFP growth to changes in the frontier leader growth varies with different levels of each structural variables. The red triangle refers to the estimated frontier spillover effect associated with a 2% MFP growth at the frontier for Australia. The label "Minimum" (Maximum) indicates the country with the lowest (highest) value for the given structural variable. Participation in GVCs is based on the OECD TiVA database, and is defined as the sum of the share of imported inputs in the overall exports of a country and of its exported goods and services used as imported inputs to produce other countries' exports. Efficiency of skill allocation is defined as the percentage of workers who are either over- or under- skilled and managerial quality refers to the average of proficiency scores (in literacy) of managers. Both measures are derived from the OECD, Survey of Adult Skills (2012). Business R&D is defined as the ratio of business R&D expenditures to value added and sourced from OECD, Main Science and Technology Indicators.
Source: Saia, A., D. Andrews and S. Albrizio (2015), "Public Policy and Spillovers from the Global Productivity Frontier Industry Level Evidence", OECD Economics Department Working Papers, No. 1238.

StatLink 🔗 *http://dx.doi.org/10.1787/888933456950*

Productivity-enhancing innovation can strengthen inclusiveness

The impact of innovation on inclusiveness depends on the specific nature of the innovation. Some recent technologies have proved to be skill biased, "scaling up" the returns to some (already) high-pay segments of the labour market. Also, the tendency for innovation to cluster can contribute to regional inequalities (OECD, 2015b). Policy should not necessarily discourage such processes, not least as the innovative products and services generated can bring wide benefits. However, policy should remain aware of inequality-widening mechanisms and ameliorate the effects where feasible. To a degree this is already a feature of policy agendas, including in Australia. Prominent examples in recent years being concern about the generosity of executive-pay packages and measures to curb base erosion and profit shifting by multinational corporations (many of which are highly innovative).

Meanwhile, some forms of productivity-enhancing innovation policies can help tackle poverty and social exclusion, playing a supportive role to core welfare policy. Australia's most prominent welfare challenge remains the large socio-economic gaps between aboriginal communities (particularly those in remote areas) and the rest of the population. The potential policy options bear some similarity to the innovation policies used to help resolve poverty in developing economies. A recent OECD study (OECD, 2015c) recommends that in a developing country context, policy should: steer institutional research towards innovations that will also help the poor; ensure that regulation does not stand in the way of innovation that would assist the poor; and encourage grass-roots innovation among poor communities. In the Australian context, ensuring that the menu of targeted support for aboriginal communities has innovative elements along these lines could be a useful addition to the wide-ranging measures already in place. In addition, ensuring access to good ICT services is particularly relevant (see below) as this facilitates that rural communities benefit from (and contribute to) ICT-related innovation.

Innovation policy can be inclusive in a broader sense by favouring innovation processes that bring benefits to the population at large. Australian policy already does this, albeit often implicitly. Government often backs research in areas with potential for significant return to the public but which are unattractive to the private sector (for instance, because the innovation is inherently hard to appropriate or for which there are no identifiable financial revenue streams). Research in some areas of health care and innovations in education are prime examples.

Innovation policy can be infused by additional strategic elements to boost societal benefits further. In particular through:

- Re-evaluation of innovation-support mechanisms with a view strengthening their potential contribution to wider society. Public-return dimensions can be built more formally into the mechanisms themselves. For example, grant-allocation processes can explicitly give higher profile to projects with potential to benefit wider society, especially low-to-middle income households.

- Recognition of "low-tech" innovation. Low-tech innovation is often associated with the search for simple, low-cost solutions to problems faced by developing countries. However, developed countries can benefit from this approach too. For instance, low-tech (or perhaps "middle"-tech) innovation in production processes in traditional manufacturing sectors can sometimes facilitate the retention of jobs and communities.

- Ensuring good ICT connectivity and user know-how. Given the current wave of internet-based innovation, it is important to ensure the population at large has the means (and know-how) to tap into the new services coming on stream, and opportunity to participate in the innovation process.

Specific policy issues for Australia

Federal and state governments can strengthen innovation-driven productivity growth in numerous ways. The rest of this chapter considers issues that are particularly relevant for Australia.

- First, there are policy areas that broadly influence the operating environment across practically all types of firm and sectors:

  ❖ **Competition and flexible markets**. Ensuring competitive and flexible product and labour service markets is particularly important in Australia. The country's geography separates markets, compromising competition for goods, services and labour. While Australia's regulatory and policy frameworks are already relatively flexible and supportive, further improvement would enhance the economy's ability to absorb innovation and increase the share of businesses operating at the frontiers of technology and best-practice.

  ❖ **Firm dynamics.** Ensuring institutional and regulatory settings encourage allocative efficiency, and so bringing more firms close to innovation frontiers through the entry, exit, expansion and contraction of firms is as significant for Australia as elsewhere.

- Second, there are policy areas that target specific aspects of business innovation:
  - ❖ **Support for small and medium enterprises (SMEs)**. Australia has a wide-ranging menu of support schemes for SMEs, many of them aiming to encourage innovation; ensuring this support is efficient and effective is key.
  - ❖ **Intellectual property (IP)**. Products and services protected by copyright, patents and other forms of IP are becoming increasingly significant; making sure that these arrangements are efficient and serve the interests of the Australian economy is particularly relevant at the present time.
  - ❖ **Internet-platform "disruptors"**. Ensuring appropriate integration of "disruptive" services will be important for ensuring Australian households and businesses benefit from this new wave of innovation.
  - ❖ **Information and communication technology (ICT).** Access to low cost, high-speed telecommunication is critical to households' and businesses' ability to tap into much of today's innovation; ICT-related innovation is still playing out, for instance many believe that the "Internet of Things" will bring a new wave of innovation. For Australia, bringing ICT to remote areas is particularly challenging.
- Third, policy has considerable influence in determining the "human capital" for innovation through **education and skills**. Similar to many other countries Australian education policy has been favouring subjects perceived as of greatest relevance to today's innovation (notably science, technology, engineering and mathematics, i.e. STEM) and is encouraging individuals to think in innovative and entrepreneurial ways.
- Finally, governments can work towards productivity improvement through **innovation in public services**. A substantial share of Australia's labour and capital inputs are devoted to public services, encouraging innovation in the sector can ramp up cost-effectiveness and service quality with positive impact on well-being for many households.

Promoting competition and flexible markets

Competition should be a central theme in improving Australia's capacity for innovation. Current research (e.g. Aghion, 2014) emphasises that competition motivates innovation especially among firms at the technological frontier as innovation provides commercial advantage (the "escape-competition effect"). This suggests policy that both encourages strong competition and takes measures that increase the share of firms operating at technological frontiers is particularly powerful.

Australia's geography conspires against competition as most economic activity takes place in a small number of urban conurbations that are distant from each other and a long way from major world markets. This has consequences:

- Product and service markets are fragmented, weakening the strength of competition. Modern communications and progress in reducing barriers created by different sets of legislation and regulation across states have lessened this problem but Australia's "big distances" nevertheless remain an issue.
- Similarly, the labour market is also fragmented to an extent; moving jobs between the main urban centres generally means moving house too. This limits the capacity for reallocation of labour resources.

- "Upscaling challenges" in trade arise. Trade facilitates the diffusion and adoption of innovation, but involves fixed costs, which imply businesses have to reach a certain size before embarking on international trade. Attaining sufficient scale to trade is tough for Australian firms because the domestic market as a whole is comparatively small and is compromised further by the domestic balkanisation of markets. Policy can counter this, for instance by ensuring that regulation and policy settings do not hinder firm growth.

Reform to competition legislation and enforcement continues

The latest initiative to improve Australia's competition legislation and frameworks, the Harper Review (Harper et al., 2015), has recommended a number of reforms, of which the following are being pursued:

- Institutional reform that enhances the role of the strategic body in competition policy. Following the Harper Review, the government reaffirmed the role of the "executive" authority (the Australian Competition and Consumer Commission, ACCC) and aims to strengthen the role of the "strategic" authority (currently the National Competition Council, NCC). The reinvigorated strategic authority is expected to play a key role in monitoring of progress in reform and recommendations on policy design.

- Alignment of the legislative treatment of dominant firms with international norms. Currently, Australia's (and New Zealand's) treatment of dominant firms is unusual. Abuse of dominant position is prohibited only if a firm "takes advantage" of its market power for the purpose of eliminating or substantially damaging a competitor, or preventing or deterring competitive conduct. Framing the law around intent is problematic (for example proving the purpose of commercial conduct is tricky) and the Review recommended adding a mechanism that brings firms under scrutiny based on the effect of commercial conduct on competition (an "effects test") (Harper et al, 2015). In 2016 the government drafted legislation amending the relevant section of competition law (Section 46).

As the relative merits of different institutional arrangements in competition policy depend very much on context, there is no strong international guidance on the exact split between executive powers and strategic powers. Meanwhile, the alterations to how dominant firms are defined in law looks to bring Australia more in line with other jurisdictions. Stronger abuse of dominance provisions will bolster firm dynamics in particular by reducing the incidence of incumbent dominant firms harming competition in specific markets. Continuing the implementation of the Harper Review remains the key task for competition-legislation reform.

Product-market regulation is in reasonable shape

Australia's product-market regulation is, overall, fairly light. Its score in the OECD's product-market regulation index is good (Figure 1.6). This is echoed in the World Bank's *Doing Business* indicator where Australia currently ranks 10th best within the OECD area. However, Australia's lead in this respect has narrowed over time as other countries have caught up. Re-gaining that lead could usefully boost Australia's competitiveness.

Regulations on international trade can limit the absorption of new innovation. As regards foreign direct investment, which can be a core channel for importing new technologies, Australia's policy is generally geared towards encouraging such flows. However concerns about some forms of inward investment have recently led to alterations

Figure 1.6. **Australia's lead in lighter product market regulation has narrowed**

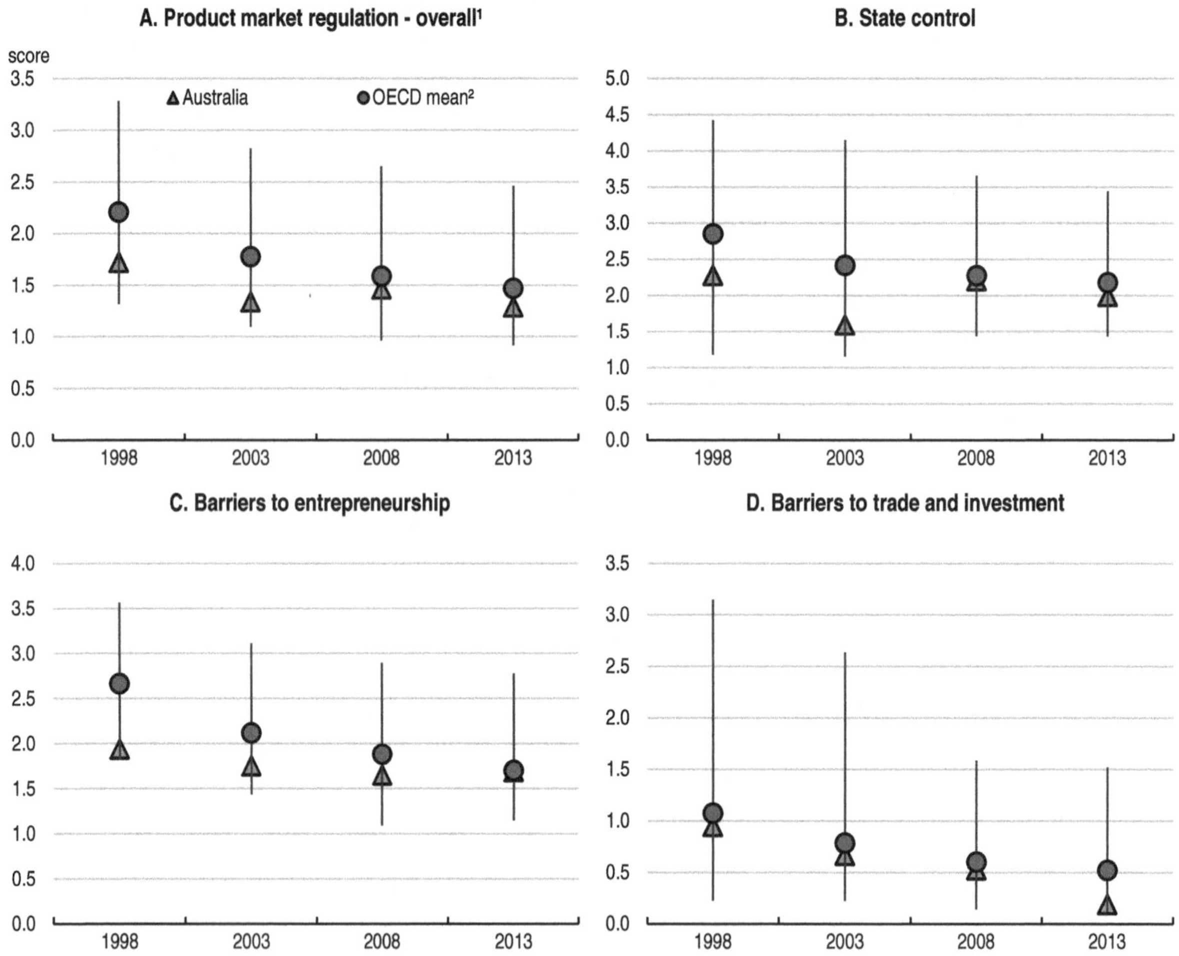

A. Product market regulation - overall[1]

B. State control

C. Barriers to entrepreneurship

D. Barriers to trade and investment

1. Scores potentially range from zero to 6 and increase with restrictiveness.
2. OECD mean is depicted on a line connecting the minimum and maximum values within OECD.
Source: OECD (2015), "Economy-wide regulation", OECD Product Market Regulation Statistics (database).
StatLink 〓〓 http://dx.doi.org/10.1787/888933456965

to the foreign-investment regulations (see Box 1.3). Developed economies, including Australia, are broadly open to services trade; scores on OECD's Services Trade Restrictiveness index are generally good (Figure 1.7). However, most of Australia's least favourable scores relate to transportation and logistics, which probably link to the country's particular problems in generating competition in among ports and airports, with again geography being a factor.

Data suggest documentary compliance for the imports and export of goods may be a specific problem for Australia. In the World Bank's sub-indicator on this issue Australia ranks 32nd in the OECD area and details show substantial time and money costs on both exporting and importing processes. Figure 1.8 shows that the average time to complete border compliance for exports is 36 hours in Australia compared with less than 15 hours among other OECD high-income countries. Discussions with the authorities in preparation for this review on this issue did not resolve whether these indicators are flagging a genuine issue or otherwise. The indicator on export compliance is based on the case of a single representative export good and trading partner for each country. Therefore it is possible

---

Box 1.3. **Australia's fee on foreign investment applications**

In November 2015 Australia introduced a fee payable for all foreign investment applications at the time of application (Foreign Acquisitions and Takeovers Fees Imposition Act 2015). The fee varies depending on the type of investment (business acquisitions, commercial land, agricultural land or residential land) and on the size of the investment. It ranges from AUD 5 000 (in the case of an investment of less than a million AUD in agricultural or residential land) to AUD 101 500 (in the case of an investment of more than a billion AUD in businesses).

According to the Australian authorities, the measure helps fund the administrative costs related to the country's investment review system.

This fee, together with the introduction of a AUD 55 million screening threshold for foreign investment in Australian agribusiness and a reduction in the foreign investment screening thresholds in agricultural land, are currently being assessed under Australia's obligations as an Adherent to the OECD Code of Liberalisation of Capital Movement, an OECD legally binding instrument and an international standard for capital account liberalisation.

Figure 1.7. **Australia's services trade is least open in transport-related sectors**

OECD Service Trade Restrictiveness Index, 2015

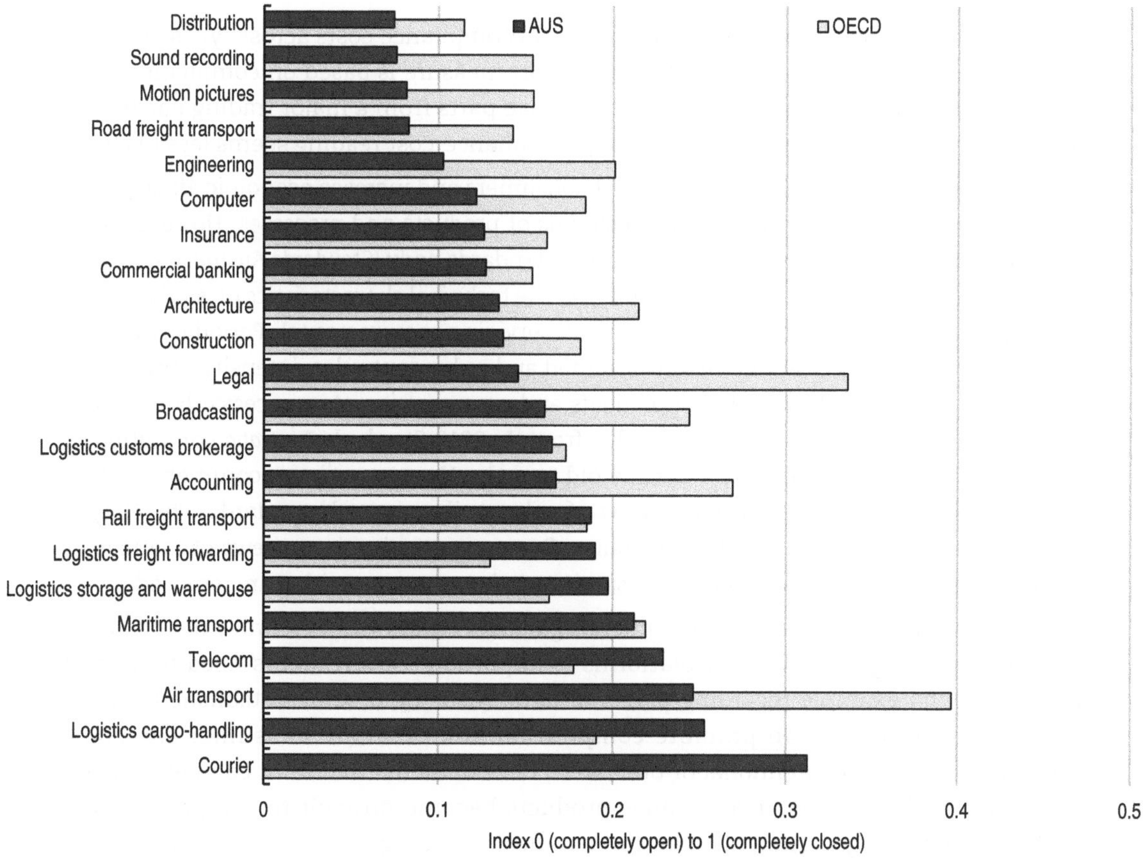

Index 0 (completely open) to 1 (completely closed)

Source: OECD (2015), Services Trade Restrictiveness Index.

StatLink http://dx.doi.org/10.1787/888933456972

Figure 1.8. **Indicators suggest Australia's export and import compliance costs may be heavy**

Doing Business Indicators: Trading Across Borders, 2017[1]

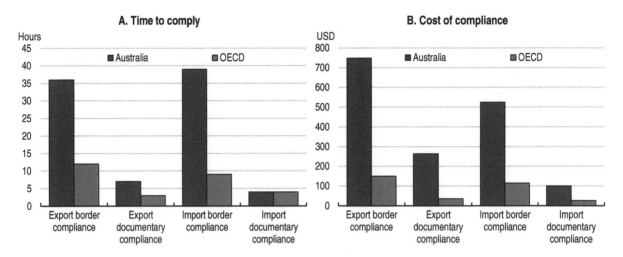

1. The indicators measure the time and cost (excluding tariffs) associated with exporting and importing a shipment of goods to and from the economy's main trading partner. For Australia, considered are export of meat and edible meat offal to Japan and import of parts and accessories of motor vehicles from United States.

Source: World Bank (2016), Doing Business 2017: Equal Opportunity for All.

StatLink ⬛⬛⬛ *http://dx.doi.org/10.1787/888933456983*

that cross-country variation reflects differences in compliance costs across types of goods, not differences in country compliance. The import measure is based on compliance costs for the importation of a common set of automotive parts from a major trading partner, so a technical explanation for Australia's heavy compliance-cost reading seems less likely.

Technical standards can usefully protect consumers and increase economic efficiency by providing uniform and transparent specifications of products and processes. However, such standards can be too invasive. Australia's goods' standards body (*Standards Australia*) manages around 6 800 sets of rules (most are voluntary) on the technical characteristics of goods or rules relating to other product dimensions (such as servicing requirements). Periodic review of standards can usefully clear out the unwarranted and redundant rules, intensify competition and ensure that the diffusion of new products and processes is not unnecessarily impeded. There have been welcome initiatives on this front. In 2012 *Standards Australia* committed to reviewing standards more than a decade old and the Harper review recommended that *Standards Australia* initiate periodic review of voluntarily adopted standards. The Harper Review also recommended that the Australian Government prioritise reviews of mandatory product standards to ensure that unnecessary restrictions on competition are removed.

Finally, ensuring consumer-protection regulation covers the new wave of consumer services emerging from internet platforms is important. Governments need to protect consumers, for example regarding personal data. Also, as in some established service sectors, governments can promote competition and facilitate consumer choice by remaining vigilant to (intentional or otherwise) developments that limit competition and consumer choice, for instance because products become difficult to compare. Where problems develop, governments can, for instance, encourage common or standardised elements in the presentation and design of services on offer.

In sum, though Australia has good product-market regulation in general, there is a need for continued progress in weeding out superfluous regulation.

Boosting the allocative efficiency of labour resources to counter geographic disadvantage

According to a recent OECD study (McGowan and Andrews, 2015), Australia has a high rate of skill mismatch (Figure 1.9), which suggests that the allocative efficiency of labour resources is compromised. As described above, Australia's large distances between main population centres are almost certainly playing a role. However this may not be the only factor. Despite past progress in narrowing gaps, inter-state differences in education and vocational training systems may still be hindering labour mobility. Further progress on this front would help (for example by work in ensuring mutual recognition of state-based vocational qualifications). OECD empirical work (Figure 1.10) on factors driving skill mismatch suggests Australia would also benefit from making housing supply more responsive.

Figure 1.9. **Skill mismatch is comparatively high in Australia**
Percentage of qualification-mismatched workers[1]

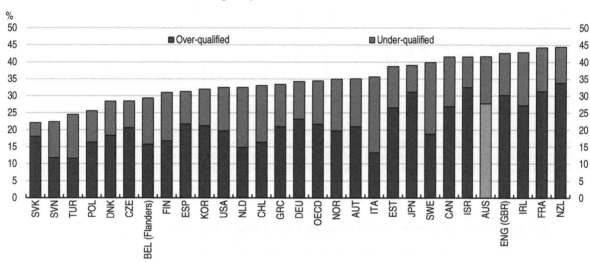

1. Qualifications mismatch arises when workers have an educational attainment that is higher or lower than that required by their job. If their qualification level is higher than that required by their job, workers are classified as overqualified; if the opposite is true, they are classified as underqualified. In the Survey of Adult Skills, workers are asked what would be the usual qualifications, if any, "that someone would need to get (their) type of job if applying today". The answer to this question is used as each worker's qualification requirements and compared to their actual qualifications to identify mismatch. While biased by individual perceptions and period or cohort effects, self-reported qualification requirements along these lines have the advantage of being job-specific rather than assuming that all jobs with the same occupational code require the same level of qualifications.

Source: OECD (2016), Skills Matter: Further Results from the Survey of Adult Skills.

StatLink 🔗 *http://dx.doi.org/10.1787/888933456999*

Improving resource reallocation through firm dynamics

Firm dynamics – the entry, exit, expansion and contraction of businesses – to a large extent reflect how easily resources can be relocated in an economy. Improved firm dynamics can boost innovation-based productivity through resource-allocation processes. Flexible product and labour-market settings and strong market competition (discussed above) contribute to efficient resource reallocation. However, there are also more proximate policy influences on firm dynamics. The following sections examine: administrative procedures and regulatory requirements on business ("red tape") and insolvency legislation and procedures.

Figure 1.10. **Policy reforms can help reduce skill mismatches**

Probability of mismatch for different values of the policy variables

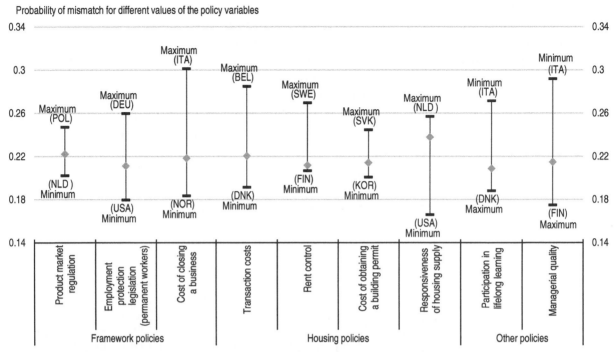

Note: The probability of mismatch for different values of the policy variables is based on a probit analysis that included a range of control variables as well as those shown in the figure. The distance between the minimum and maximum indicates the range of probability across the data used in the analysis according to the coefficients generated by the probit analysis.
Source: Adalet McGowan, M and D. Andrews (2015), "Skill Mismatch and Public Policy in OECD countries", OECD Economics Department Working Paper, No. 1210.

StatLink ᴹˢᴾ http://dx.doi.org/10.1787/888933457005

Red tape associated with establishing and operating a business

Red tape can hinder the development of businesses. Indeed, evidence suggests start-ups are more exposed than incumbents to this aspect of the policy environment (OECD, 2016a). Australia compares favourably as regards procedures required for establishing a business. The "entrepreneurship" component of the OECD's product market indicator indicates low barriers to firm entry. Also, Australia ranks 11th highest out of 189 economies in the "Starting a Business" component of the World Bank's *Doing Business* indicator. There are nevertheless avenues for improvement. For example, the Productivity Commission's recent report on business entry and exit (Productivity Commission, 2015) suggests:

● Strengthening the implementation of best practice in business regulation at all levels of government. There have been several official investigations and reports providing guidance on regulatory best practice; according to the Commission the priority is now to encourage application of them.

● Expedition of land-tenure reform. There are several categories of land-tenure in Australia coupled with state-by-state variation in specific arrangements. Also, a property can be subject to overlapping tenure arrangements. These complications principally affect businesses in rural and remote areas.

Tuning insolvency legislation to better support innovation and risk taking

Insolvency legislation and procedure affect innovation because they influence behaviour, including risk taking, by businesses (the "debtors") and those financing them (the "creditors"). A recent review (McGowan and Andrews, 2016) underscores that insolvency systems need to offer opportunity to restructure and, where necessary, facilitate exit predictably and expediently (Box 1.4). The *National Innovation and Science Agenda* has welcomed proposals to alter current corporate insolvency arrangements to better encourage risk taking and entrepreneurship. The corporate insolvency measures comprise (Government of Australia, 2016):

● Introduction of a safe harbour from personal liability for insolvent trading, which would allow company directors to retain control of the company (instead of ceding control to an external advisor) if the company is undertaking a restructure.

● Making "ipso facto" clauses, which allow contracts to be terminated due to an insolvency event, unenforceable if the company is undertaking a restructure.

These proposals for lighter regulation for creditors should be implemented. Past policy work has done much to smooth the path for firm entry; attention now needs to turn to firm exit.

Box 1.4. **Key elements of insolvency**

A recent OECD review of insolvency (McGowan and Andrews, 2016) underscores that there is no single best-practice model of insolvency due to the wide variation in institutional and legislative contexts across countries. However some key elements appear to be critical:

● A clear trigger for initiating insolvency proceedings that encourages early remedial action towards restructuring

● Efficient liquidation options and fair opportunity for rehabilitation

● Checks against undesirable strategic behaviour

● Options for out-of-court settlement

● Provisions for cross-border insolvency and equal treatment for foreign and domestic creditors

● Attention to personal insolvency arrangements so that these align with the objectives of corporate insolvency

---

Ensuring SME support is efficient and effective

Many of Australia's SME-support schemes endeavour to aid innovative enterprises. Economic arguments for such support can include a need to address disadvantages for SMEs that arise through informational asymmetries or market failures, or a view that there are public returns to SME-based entrepreneurial risk-taking that justify additional subsidy.

Policy targeting and efficiency is a core challenge for SME support. As pointed out in the Productivity Commission's report covering firm entry and exit (Productivity Commission, 2015), Australia has comparable churn of SME entries and exits to other countries. However (as elsewhere) only a small proportion of SMEs are innovative and within these only a fraction will thrive. Furthermore, SMEs are heterogeneous, as they play a role in practically all sectors of the economy. A long menu of support schemes has developed, each programme or measure targeting a particular type of SME business, or activity. A recent investigation by federal government found there to be 256 State and Territory programmes and 83 federal-government measures that aimed to boost innovation, most aimed at the SME sector. Recent proposals for schemes (Table 1.1) include a tax break for investors in small business, additional support for venture capital financing and a special fund to support biomedical companies transition from early to late stage research.

Table 1.1. **Recent measures to support innovative SMEs**

Initiative	Selected detail
Tax Incentives for Early Stage (Angel) Investors	• Concessional tax treatment for investors (as of July 2016) includes a 20% non-refundable tax offset capped at AUD 200 000 per year and a 10-year capital gains tax exemption for investments held for at least twelve months • Eligibility conditions for the enterprise (as of July 2016) include expenditure and income limits (AUD 1 million and AUD 200 000 respectively)
New Arrangements for Venture Capital Limited Partnerships	Partners in new Early Stage Venture Capital Limited Partnerships (ESCCLPs) are eligible for the following concessions (as of July 2016): • A 10% non-refundable tax offset on capital invested • An increase in maximum fund size from AUD 100 million to AUD 200 million • No requirement for funds to divest if a company's value exceeds AUD 250 million
Biomedical Translation Fund	This government-financed fund facilitates firms transition between early and late stage biomedical research (the so-called "valley of death"). Specifically, the fund is being financed by redirecting initial capital contributions from the Medical Research Future Fund (MRFF). This will make investment available earlier than it would have otherwise been under the MRFF. The Fund will not impact the target of achieving a balance of AUD 20 billion in the MRFF by 2019-20.

Improving the effectiveness menu of SME-support programmes can be facilitated by:

● Stronger programme oversight, review and reform processes to identify and remove underperforming programmes, build on successful programmes and encourage policy experimentation.

● Ensuring awareness of the programmes on offer among prospective start-ups and existing SMEs.

Though SME support endeavours to nurture innovation and business success, it can in fact hold some firms back by discouraging upscaling. By definition, the programmes incorporate size-based eligibility criteria, based on dimensions such as the value of business turnover or the number of employees (Table 1.2). The increased focus on supporting SMEs in recent government policy, such as the introduction of a lower rate of corporate tax for the sector will add further to dissuading transition to larger-scale operations.

Overall, Australia needs to strengthen review and reform mechanisms for SME support, taking into account that support can discourage firms' expansion. Ensuring good awareness of schemes by firms is also important.

Table 1.2. **Examples of size-criteria in SME support**

Type of SME support	Examples of specific support mechanisms
Federal tax concessions	Since 2015-16 the concessionary rate of corporate income tax (28.5% instead of 30%) has applied to companies with less than AUD 2 million in turnover In the R&D Tax Incentive program, firms with less than AUD 20 million turnover are entitled to a 43.% refundable tax offset, compared with the a non-refundable tax offset of 38.5% for all other eligible entities
Federal grant schemes targeting specific issues or sectors	Export Market Development Grant. Targets firms with income of less than AUD 50 million Textile, Clothing, Footwear Small Business Programme. Targets firms with fewer than 20 employees
State tax support and similar	Payroll tax concessions for small business in South Australia are limited to companies with payroll below AUD 1.2 million

Ensuring intellectual property legislation rewards innovation without compromising diffusion

Intellectual property (IP) legislation provides property rights to innovators, helping them generate a return on their inventions or ideas. However, policy design is challenging, in particular the balancing between providing commercial reward through property rights for innovators against the risk that this can limit diffusion and hinder further innovation. Also, scope for unilateral reform by individual governments is limited because many dimensions of IP are set by international agreements.

A recent draft Productivity Commission report (Productivity Commission, 2016a) reviews Australia's IP regime (Table 1.3). It provides a welcome top-down perspective, emphasising core principles, such as additionality. A central conclusion of the report is that Australia's IP arrangements have swung too far in favour of the rights holders, i.e. IP protection provides excessive reward to innovators in relation to the social value of their innovations, and means higher prices for products and services and slower dissemination of innovation. Favouring weaker IP protection to a degree reflects the

Table 1.3. **Notable elements of the Productivity Commission's draft report on Intellectual Property (released April 2016)**

Area of reform	Notable elements of the Commission's report
Patents	The report advocates: More stringent patent-approval criteria Scrapping of a "second tier" patent system for SMEs Redesign of pharmaceutical-patent extensions More limited business-method and software patents
Copyright	The report calls for a new system of user rights that takes a more principles-based "fair use" approach, giving courts more leeway in determining when copyright goes not apply (the current system comprises a list of exemptions that can only be altered through legislative change). The report says that calls for stronger "geoblocking" of internet content should be resisted. Currently, the practice of circumnavigating geoblocking by consumers (for example through proxy servers) does not represent an infringement of Australia's copyright system
Enforcement	With a view to assist SMEs, efforts to develop low-cost informal channels for resolving IP issues in the federal court system should continue The report concludes that the case for a separate IP court structure (such as in the UK) is not clear, the benefits of such a system can probably be replicated within the current structure
IP rights and competition policy	Competition law should apply more broadly to IP; specifically the report proposes the scrapping of "section 51(3)" which provides partial exemption in the licensing and assignment of IP
Multilateral and bilateral trade agreements	The report advocates: That government's seek "more balanced" arrangements for patents and copyright and lower transactions and administrative costs for parties seeking IP rights in multiple jurisdictions Improving the evidence base and analysis that informs international agreement

(understandable) self-interest of a net-importer of innovation. Other countries in a similar position to Australia probably make similar cases, and, meanwhile, net IP exporters argue for the reverse; IP protection has much akin with trade negotiation.

The Productivity Commission's report also makes many practical recommendations for improving less controversial aspects of IP. The report makes a convincing case for scrapping a second-tier patent system, which aims to assist SMEs but has proven largely ineffective. Also, the report's questioning of IP protection for business methods resonates with expert opinion globally. In sum, there appears plenty of room to "tidy up" the IP regime.

Facilitating internet-platform "disruptors"

Echoing global developments, Australia is experiencing a wave of new business models (so called disruptors), notably ride sharing and short-term accommodation (discussed below), centred on the innovative use of internet platforms (for a general discussion see OECD, 2015d). Disruption can potentially bring benefits to many households (or businesses) and make an appreciable difference to well-being. With this in mind, policy needs to embrace disruption by leaning against attempts to hobble or exclude them by incumbents and by tackling unintended obstacles to legislation and regulation.

However, disruption should not be embraced unconditionally. Policy needs to check for downsides for consumers and employees in what disruptors are offering. Policy also needs to establish whether the disruption marks a positive innovation or whether it, for example, is founded on regulatory or tax loopholes.

Ensuring competition policy supports disruption appropriately

Incumbent firms can impede disruption by either i) anti-competitive practices designed to stifle market entry; or ii) by acquisition of disruptive innovation with a view to mothballing it (De Steel and Larouche, 2015). Against the former, competition authorities should aim to keep markets open, acting quickly to prevent practices such as "defensive leveraging" (using a powerful position in one segment of a business to protect another) or extensive use of IP protection to prevent market access. Measures combatting the acquisition problem can comprise additional merger thresholds (based on a discrepancy between transaction value and turnover) or alteration of rules regarding the acquisition of "maverick firms" to better incorporate disruptors. However, policy also needs to remain vigilant to competition implications of the disruptors themselves, particularly those based on in internet platforms where strong network effects mean a single enterprise can rapidly become dominant.

General competition law provides the main instrument to combat anti-competitive practices aimed at shutting out disruptors. Here, as discussed above, a key policy issue for Australia is the legal definition of market dominance (the "Section 46" issue discussed the section on competition law above). As regards mergers, the current legislation prohibits acquisition if this substantially lessens competition (or is likely to do so), thus, in principle, providing legal means to prevent innovations being mothballed through mergers.

Clearly, Australia, as elsewhere, potentially faces stiff resistance to disruption and has to ensure competition policy counters undesirable strategies by incumbents. The role of competition law in this latest wave of market disruption should be monitored as experience deepens; general competition law may not prove a sufficient shield against anti-competitive behaviour.

Ensuring taxation and subsidy systems treat incumbents and disruptors fairly

Policy needs to ensure that tax and subsidy systems neither block disruptors nor, conversely, give them undue advantage over incumbents. Australian tax law does not expressly treat participants in the "sharing economy" separately, which is sound. Nevertheless issues can arise, and so far the tax authorities' approach to accommodation and personal-transport services indicates that a sensible case-by-case approach is being taken.

In the market for accommodation, hotels and short-term lets are subject to different treatment regarding the Goods and Services Tax (GST; Australia's value-added tax). However there are some mitigating factors that suggest this does not require policy attention. As do many VAT systems, Australia has a general rule that GST does not apply to residential rents, and this includes short-term rents arranged through apps. Meanwhile, other forms for accommodation are subject to GST. Prima facie this suggests the playing field is tilted in favour of short-term renters. However, hoteliers are able to claim GST credits on costs (whereas short-term renters cannot). Also most short-term rentals are not operating as enterprises and their rental income is taxed under the income-tax system rather than the corporate-tax system, which is the typical case for hoteliers. In any case, introducing GST on rentals would probably involve considerable compliance costs.

Meanwhile in the personal-transport sector the tax authorities are requiring providers of "ride-sourcing services" to register for GST regardless of their turnover. This is consistent with the notion that Uber drivers (or similar) and taxi drivers are competing in the same market and therefore ought to be treated equally from a tax perspective.

Sector-specific regulation: states are adopting a "cohabitation" model in ride-sharing

Sector-specific regulation can be a key blockage to disruption. The design and enforcement of such regulation can be heavily influenced by incumbents and typically there are ways of disguising protectionism as legitimate causes, such as health and safety or consumer and employee protection. To date, challenges to taxi services by ride-share companies such as Uber have been among the most prominent internet-platform based disruptions. Ride-sharing first started operating in Australia in May 2014 when Uber began operating services in Sydney. Services in other capitals followed, even though at the time there was no regulation and, strictly speaking, the services were illegal.

As in many other countries, taxi services in Australia are controlled by licencing, price regulation and other rules, many of which addressing service-quality and safety concerns for taxi users. Control of the number of taxi licences by the authorities, has effectively created an asset, whose value is reflected in the market for taxi licences. Some Australian states also restrict hire-car numbers by selling licences or imposing caps, which not only supports incumbent car-hire companies but also further protects the taxi sector.

There is much at stake in ride-share disruption for both consumers and service providers. According to one report (Minifie, 2016), spending on taxi trips amounted to AUD 5.5 billion in 2014 (i.e. around 0.3% of GDP). With a total of about 21 000 licenced taxis, this implies an average annual revenue per taxi of around AUD 260 000. Cost savings from disruption to the sector are potentially substantial. According to one estimate (Deloitte Access Economics, 2016), average taxi fares in Australia are around 25% higher than average UberX fares, which would suggest potential savings of AUS 1.4 billion based on the figure in Minifie (2016).

States have been bringing in reforms that allow both traditional taxi services and ride-sharing to coexist. To date, reforms in New South Wales and the Australian Capital Territory have been finalised (Minifie 2016). The reforms legalise ride-sharing and introduce regulatory standards for this sector but also make adjustments to the regulation of taxi services so that these can compete on an equal basis in certain segments of the market. The New South Wales reform, for instance, preserves taxi's exclusivity on "hail and rank" services and maintains fare regulation in that segment. Meanwhile, pre-booked taxi service prices are deregulated and various requirements on taxi services, such as geographic knowledge and English language removed. Meanwhile for ride-share services, there are new safety and insurance requirements.

Different approaches to compensation for taxi licence holders for loss of revenues and licence values have been taken (Figure 1.11). In New South Wales each licence holder is to receive a compensatory payment, and in addition a "hardship" fund has been established along with a buy-back scheme for licences. Meanwhile ACT's reform proposes no compensation to licence holders. Providing compensation implies the authorities are taking partial responsibility for the reduced value in taxi licences resulting from disruption to the sector. No compensation implies that the authorities believe it is reasonable for licence holders to fully bear this regulatory risk (perhaps because licence holders have benefitted positively from such risk in the past).

Figure 1.11. **Ride-sharing has prompted falls in taxi-licences values**

Taxi-license values in 2015 AUD

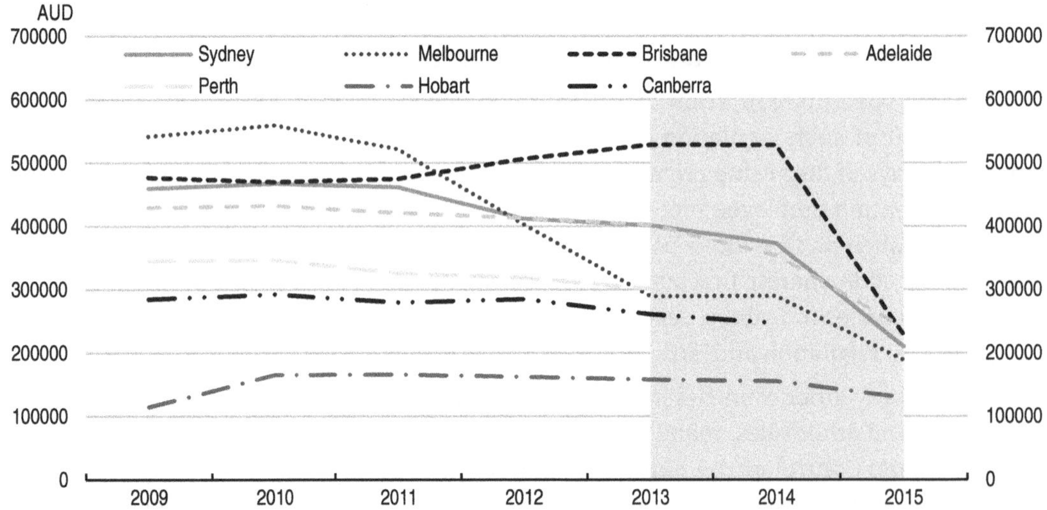

Source: Minifie, Jim & Wiltshire, Trent (2016), Peer-to-peer pressure: policy for the sharing economy, Grattan Institute.
StatLink ᵐˢᵖ http://dx.doi.org/10.1787/888933457014

Australia's state-by-state "cohabitation" reforms to accommodating ride-sharing are certainly welcome but have an element of compromise that means they fail to fully open the market to disruption. Ultimately, with suitable safety and insurance provisions the *raison d'etre* for retaining a "dual" system is weak. Retaining exclusive access for taxis such as in the "hail and rank" segment does not make a great deal of sense. In the long run the authorities should aim for no regulatory distinction between taxis and new forms of service.

Accommodation-market disruption has seen variety of regulatory responses

Short-stay rentals of houses and apartments in localities popular to tourists have taken off rapidly in Australia. Data indicate that bed spaces available via Airbnb now occupy a significant segment of the market (Figure 1.12). Statistical issues make the precise market share uncertain; some renting out accommodation post on more than one website, and many are part-time rentals. However, there is little doubt that in some localities Airbnb-type rental accommodation is making significant inroads into the accommodation market, with consequences for hoteliers, as well as the rental and housing markets.

Figure 1.12. **Australia's Airbnb market is well developed**
Number of home-sharing listings as of March 2016

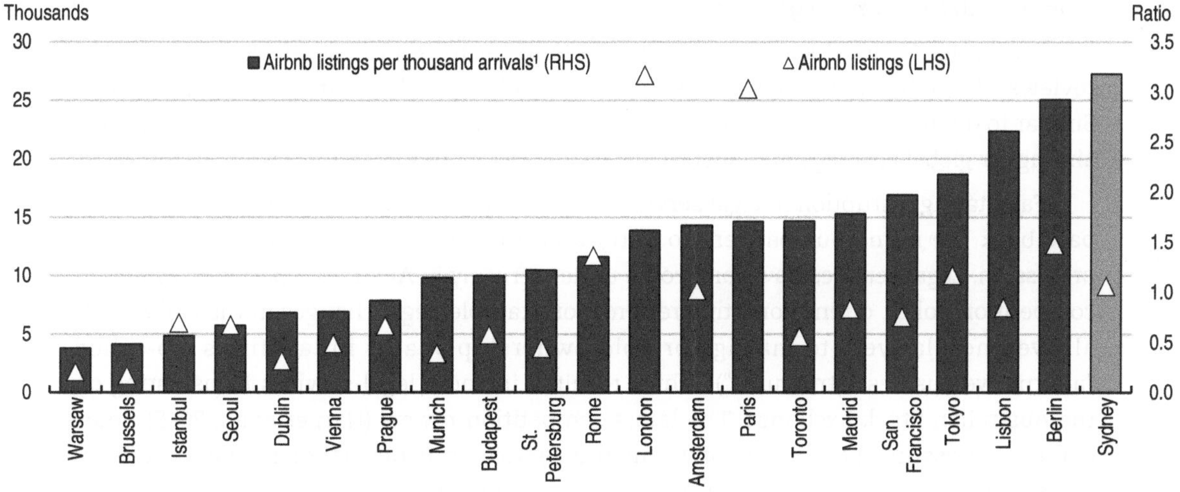

1. International tourist arrivals in 2013.
Source: Airdna (2016); Euromonitor International (2016).

StatLink ⬛ᵇ⬛ *http://dx.doi.org/10.1787/888933457020*

The regulation of short-term rentals varies widely in Australia because much of it is set by local-government. Some local governments impose fairly onerous restrictions on short-stay rentals. Similar to taxi regulation, while prima facie the rules invariably appear to address legitimate concerns, there is little doubt that commercial interests (such as hoteliers) have vigorously supported the restrictions such that the scope and depth of them may be excessive. A variety of measures are used, for instance: registration requirements, special planning approval, demonstration of compliance with building codes and limits on where short-term lets are allowed and limits on the number of guests.

Disruption to neighbours due to anti-social behaviour by short-term renters is, reportedly, fairly common in Australia's short-term let market (Minifie, 2016). This is not just a problem for neighbours but also damages the reputation of the short-term rental market. Dealing with this issue is proving tricky. The type of restrictions imposed by local government does not target the problem efficiently, imposing blanket restrictions may well fail to lessen the problem of disruption to any great extent. State laws and regulations on noise disturbance are not well suited to dealing with short-term renters. And, in addition, legislation in several states explicitly prevents owners' corporations (the bodies run by owners that manage apartment blocks) from imposing restrictions on short-term letting. Arguably, permitting such restrictions allows for granular building-by-building approach to short-term lets and would give appropriate weight to externalities on neighbours.

Australia's wide-ranging local-level regulatory response to short-term lets makes it tough to summarise and the heterogeneity is "messy". However this is not necessarily a problem to the development of the market. Most of those renting out only have to familiarise themselves with the regulations of one local government (and one state government). Arguably, the range of solutions also represents a welcome example of local democracy in action.

Over time some regulatory approaches will prove more effective than others. Encouraging the authorities (both at the state and local level) to converge to best practice as it emerges can be helped by fora to exchange experiences or by state or federal initiated assessments of the regulation with a view to setting best-practice guidelines.

Emerging disruptions: legal services

Disruption in legal services is taking several forms, online services, rankings and reviews of law firms and lawyers, service unbundling and automation (OECD, 2016b). Similar to disruption in the taxi and accommodation sectors, the new players are typically aiming for global coverage and Australia is part of the campaign trail.

Facilitating disruption in legal services chiefly requires maintaining policy pressure to pare back the numerous barriers to entry and other regulations erected by the legal profession. Legal services have long come under scrutiny in Australia's periodic reviews of competition policy, often prompting reform. For example, legal changes in the early 2000s allowed non-lawyers to manage or hold ownership shares in law firms (so-called "alternative business structures"), which resulted in some legal-services firms listing on the Australian Stock Exchange. The latest competition review (Harper et al., 2015) notes some progress in liberalising conveyancing services but nevertheless flags the legal profession along with other professions as in need of further review.

Emerging disruptions: financial services

Disruption is also underway in Australia's financial markets. Financial services differ markedly in structure from legal services in that, especially in retail products, Australia's four main banks occupy the vast majority of the market. Similar to other sectors the disruptors are often on a campaign for global presence. Recent OECD analysis (OECD, 2015e) underscores the rapid growth of new products and models. So far in Australia, as elsewhere, peer-to-peer (or peer-to-market) market lending occupies a small but rapidly growing share of the market. According to one report (KPMG, 2016) Australia's alternative finance market grew by around 320% in 2015. Also, virtual currencies, notably Bitcoin, are operating to more or less the same extent as elsewhere in the OECD area and innovative payment solutions (e.g. digital wallets) are emerging. Recent policy measures include draft legislation allowing equity crowdfunding of companies. Among the eligibility conditions crowdfunding companies must have less than AUD 25 million in assets and less than AUD 25 million per year turnover, meanwhile investors are limited to AUD 10 000 per year in any given crowdfunded company. Crowdfunding companies (if public) benefit from up to a five-year exemption on certain reporting and governance requirements.

In general, the Australian authorities are maintaining an open approach to financial-sector disruption and this is welcome. An ongoing process of assessment, regulatory adjustment and review should be maintained so that new forms of disruption can be accommodated, as appropriate. Given the uncertainties in how best to regulate new financial services, the Australia Securities and Investments Commission is developing a regulatory "sand box", similar to that introduced by the UK's Financial Conduct Authority, which would provide a legal right to business that fit certain criteria to validate their concepts without having a licence.

Also the authorities are sensibly providing information and advice on the new financial services. For instance, the Australian Securities and Investments Commission established an Innovation Hub to provide tailored information and informal assistance for new firms looking to obtain a licence and has posted information and advice for consumers on peer-to-peer (or market) lending. As with practically all financial products, there are complexities and potential pitfalls that consumers should be aware of to make good decisions.

Summing up

To-date Australian policy has, in broad terms, embraced disruption, endeavouring to reshape regulation to accommodate new players and maintain neutrality of treatment. However, incumbents have been successful in defending their interests to a degree, as seen in the reforms to accommodate ride-sharing. This will undoubtedly remain a theme, especially in areas where incumbents wield influence, legal and financial services being a case in point. Leaning against such vested interests will be key. This said disruptors' business models and associated calls for deregulation should not be embraced unconditionally. Though regulation is often ramped up and skewed to protect incumbents, the principles it is supposed to serve are often sound. Regulation needs to be stripped of incumbent bias, not necessarily removed entirely.

As pointed out in the Productivity Commission report on digital disruption (Productivity Commission, 2016b), a "wait and see" (but react quickly) approach to future disruption makes most sense. Federal and state governments need to be ready to assess and act as new business models emerge. Encouragingly the Australian Competition and Consumer Commission has established an internal working group that tracks disruption in markets and provides a vehicle for provisional assessment of the pros and cons of emerging business models and products.

Ensuring access to low cost, high speed ICT

Much of today's innovation centres on the use of information and communication technology. In particular, new innovative business models, such as for peer-to-peer accommodation or transport, depend crucially on mobile networks. As regards fixed-line networks, households and business require affordable and fast landline Internet connections to access innovative products and services. Both technologies will be critical platforms for the development of the "Internet of Things", which is seen by many as the source of much new innovation in products and services (see Box 1.5).

OECD comparisons suggest Australia's mobile services are comparatively inexpensive. The latest data indicate prices are well in the bottom half of the OECD distribution (Figure 1.13). However, broadband prices are comparatively high and penetration is low, most notably at higher speeds. For example, according to OECD data Australia has among the lowest penetration of broadband at speeds above 10 megabits per second (Figure 1.14).

Australia faces similar challenges to other countries in ensuring competitive ICT services in urban areas and, in addition, faces particularly large challenges in developing provision in rural and remote areas due to the large distances and sparseness of rural

> ### Box 1.5. **The "Internet of Things" in the Australian context**
>
> The Internet of Things refers to the connection of devices and objects to expand the network of networks. It encompasses developments in machine-to-machine communication, the cloud, big data and sensors and actuators. This convergence will widen the scope of machine learning and autonomy, as well as remote control (see the *Digital Economy Outlook*, OECD, 2015f). Households, businesses and public services in Australia are likely to see similar developments to elsewhere, with increasing roll-out of health-care devices, connected appliances, smart grids, smart buildings and houses. In addition, Australia will potentially benefit significantly from applications in rural and remote settings, such as crop or livestock monitoring systems.

Figure 1.13. **Australia's mobile telephony prices compare more favourably than its broadband prices**

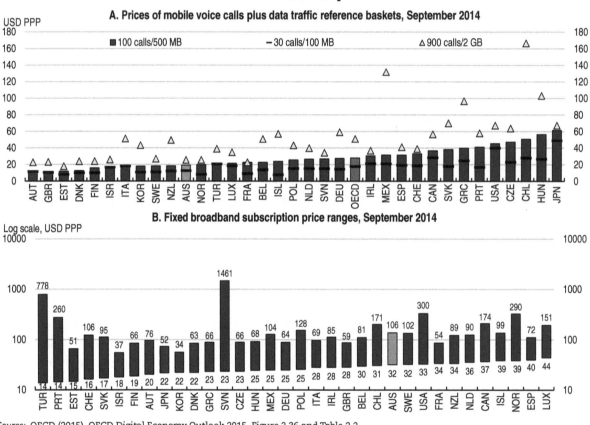

Source: OECD (2015), OECD Digital Economy Outlook 2015, Figure 2.36 and Table 2.2.

StatLink ⚍ *http://dx.doi.org/10.1787/888933457035*

populations. Though expensive, ensuring good rural access potentially brings wide benefits including improvements in public health, social engagement and education. Similar to elsewhere, and possibly to a greater degree, the machinery of government in Australia has not developed ideally for ICT policy because different segments of the sector fall under different agencies.

Figure 1.14. **Broadband speed and penetration are in the bottom half of the OECD distribution**

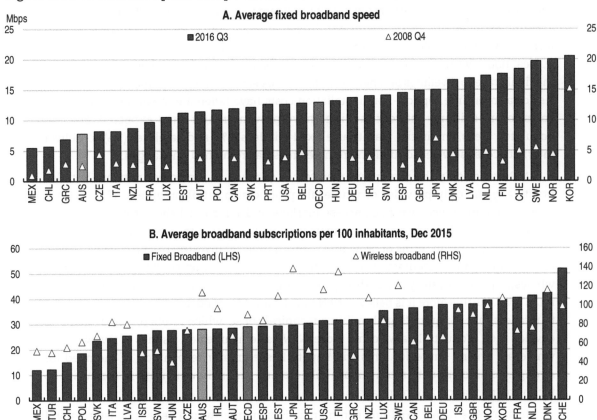

Source: Akamai (2016), State of the Internet report, Q3 2016 report; OECD, Broadband Portal, *www.oecd.org/sti/broadband/oecdbroadbandportal.htm*, February 2016.

StatLink ᴍᴸᴾ *http://dx.doi.org/10.1787/888933457049*

Fixed-line telephony: *reforms to wholesale pricing would be welcome*

Australia's fixed-line access infrastructure has undergone significant change in recent years. Previously, the incumbent, *Telstra*, controlled fixed telecommunication and cable television networks, as it was the owner and operator of the local access infrastructure, which comprises mainly the copper-based network first developed for telephony and coaxial cable for pay-television. Reforms announced in 2009 launched substantial public investment in fixed-line infrastructure and brought significant change in the architecture of the system, including the creation of a public company – the *National Broadband Network* (NBN).

NBN was primarily established as an operational body for investment in infrastructure to improve networks in urban areas and, especially, in rural areas. In urban areas, the establishment of NBN involved the incumbent, *Telstra*, allowing access to its system of conduits (so that new cabling could be installed) and agreement by *Telstra* to de-commission its copper-based network (though implementation of the latter has been put on hold following a change in the technical approach, see below). Thus, in essence reform has resulted in control of the access infrastructure network being taken away from *Telstra* and placed under the control of NBN.

The choice of technology for NBN's infrastructure investment in urban areas has been contentious. Initially an entirely optical-fibre system was envisaged for urban areas (which account for over 93% of connections). However, cost concerns resulted in a mixed-technology system. Roll-out in many urban areas now comprises the fibre network ending at local nodes with the pre-existing copper or coaxial cable networks being used to cover the final stage to dwellings and businesses. The cost savings of this approach have become less clear over time. Optical-fibre installation costs have fallen and repair and renovation costs to pre-existing network facilities have proven greater than expected. For less populated areas, the initial plan to use fixed wireless (4%) and satellites (3%) to deliver Internet access services to rural and remote areas has remained unchanged.

NBN is not only the owner and maintainer of much of the access network but also practically the only provider of wholesale products to retail providers. This gives it considerable influence over fixed access markets. Indeed, some believe NBN's wholesale pricing strategies focus heavily on using its monopoly position to maximise revenue. This might be attractive in terms of providing a return to fiscal investment, but may be forcing consolidation (and discouraging entry) in the market for internet service providers. NBN's wholesale pricing strategy is also thought to be influencing how prices are structured at the retail level. Furthermore it is believed NBN may be limiting innovation by offering products to retailers that are quite "high level" in a technical sense, which limits retailers' ability to develop their products. In a welcome move, NBN has embarked on a series of reviews of its wholesale pricing strategies. This will hopefully see greater recognition of the need for stronger retail competition to increase take-up and an environment more conducive to technical innovation among retailers.

In sum, Australia's fixed-line communications market would benefit substantially if the wholesaler (NBN) gave greater technical and pricing flexibility to retailers.

In mobile telephony a fourth retail provider would be particularly welcome

Though Australia's mobile telephony prices are not extraordinarily high in international comparison, there is room for improvement in this, and other dimensions of mobile services. Australia's mobile telephony market currently comprises the incumbent mobile-network operator (MNO), *Telstra*, and two other operators (*Optus* and *Vodaphone-Hutchison Australia* (VHA)). In addition, there are several mobile virtual network operators (MVNOs), though these have limited scope for product innovation and most use MNOs with less geographical coverage than the market leaders. Entry of a new player in 2003 (*Hutchison-3*) saw the number of competing MNOs rise to four but this ended in 2009 following a merger with *Vodaphone* to form VHA (see Table 1.4).

Some analysis (OECD, 2014b) indicates that mobile markets are substantially more competitive when there are four or more MNOs in the market compared to less than four MNOs. Various factors might explain this "four-player advantage". It could be that the nature of economies of scale and networking effects in mobile communication means three (or fewer) players can generally occupy the market without having to compete fiercely, while the fourth player has to "disrupt" the market to establish themselves. Australia's experience in moving from three MNOs to four in 2003 and back to three in 2009 provides an interesting case study. OECD (2014b) points to an end in price declines after 2009 and diminished data allowances in retail products following the reduction in

Table 1.4. **Development of Australia's mobile network operators**

Date		Number of (effective) competitors
1987	First mobile network established by the incumbent, *Telstra*	One
1992-1993	*Optus* and *Vodaphone* enter the market	Three
2003	3-G auctions prompted entry of a new operator *Hutchison-3*. *Hutchison-3*'s establishment involves a 3G network sharing agreement with *Telstra*	Four, though two in a network sharing agreement
2009	The two smallest operators *Vodaphone* and *Hutchison-3* merge to form *Vodaphone Hutchison Australia* (*VHA*), however the two brands continue to be marketed	Four retail product lines but in effect only three players
2011	*VHA* announces termination of *Hutchison-3* product line, with customers being transferred to *Vodaphone* by 2013. *VHA* ends 3G sharing agreement between *Hutchison* and *Telstra* and establishes one with *Optus*	Three retail product lines, three effective players (one network sharing agreement)

MNO competition. Also, international roaming prices remain high for many users, with "roam like at home" plans being much less developed in Australia than in countries with four MNOs (e.g. France, United Kingdom, United States).

In light of the evidence of a "four-player advantage", new entry into Australia's mobile market would be welcome. New players could precipitate innovation in mobile products and more importantly, stronger competition could bring price and quality improvements to services that facilitate the development of innovative new platforms for Internet-based services. The authorities should certainly seek to invite and advocate new entry into the market (for example when selling off radio-wave spectrum), make technical and other regulation conducive to the development of the Internet of Things market and ensure that public investment does not entrench existing market power.

Introducing greater flexibility in access to mobile networks is currently a key issue for regulators. In most countries, including Australia, only MNOs are licensed to issue the special access numbers ("international mobile subscriber identity", IMSIs) that provide access to mobile networks. Furthermore, these numbers are generally physically stored on MNO-dedicated cards ("subscriber identity modules", SIM cards). Therefore users are effectively locked into a single MNO network (with its various coverage and pricing characteristics), unless they sign up for more than one MNO and switch SIM cards. Regulators need to promote greater flexibility. Belgium and the Netherlands recently introduced provisions to allow additional entities (such as a car manufacturer wishing to embed mobile access in cars) the right to their own IMSI numbers. Such changes would facilitate seamless hand off from one network to another, which is likely to become increasingly important as the Internet of Things develops.

Additional measures could be taken to address Australia's challenges with rural-area coverage. The latest *Regional Telecommunications Review* (Government of Australia, 2015) underscores continuing challenges regarding highway coverage, access for agricultural communities (especially in light of new sensing and tracking technologies becoming available in agriculture) and emergency services. As one MNO in Australia has superior network coverage and there is network sharing by the two smaller players there is less competition in rural areas. There may be opportunities for further leveraging the NBN investment, using a system of towers that transmit broadband wireless services to rooftop dishes. Potentially, these towers and the fixed lines connecting them could be made available to retail mobile providers to extend choice and coverage in rural areas. In addition, the restrictions on the use of domestic cellular base stations (such as "femtocells") should be examined with a view to these providing greater coverage and reducing switching costs. Both these measures could make a substantial improvement in the competitiveness of Australia's mobile telephony market in rural areas.

In sum, new entrants should be sought in mobile telephony markets and solutions to rural coverage encouraged (for example by using towers being installed for broadband).

Education and skills for innovation: what special measures can be taken?

Education and training ("human capital" development) fundamentally influence the capacity of economies to create, adapt and absorb innovation. Australia's comparatively high living standards and levels of productivity provide broad testimony to the scope and quality of the education system. Also, more immediate indicators, such as the OECD's PISA test, point to an above-average performance. Furthermore, efforts to improve the system continue with ongoing implementation of a multi-year reform to primary and secondary education and efforts to tackle issues in the vocational education and training system (see discussion in the Assessment and Recommendations of this review).

In addition to efforts for broad improvement in the education system, targeted measures can be used to tackle specific innovation issues. This approach is exemplified in proposals in the *National Innovation and Science Agenda* which contains proposals to increase student interest in ICT, as well as science, technology, engineering and maths (STEM) skills and encourage more women to engage in science and technology related careers. The programmes mainly target primary and secondary schooling (see Box 1.6).

Box 1.6. **Education programmes proposed in the *National Innovation and Science Agenda***

ICT skills. *Embracing the digital age.* A five-year programme (costed at AUD 51 million) for primary and secondary education including support for teachers to teach digital technologies, ICT summer schools and online computing challenges.

STEM skills, *Inspiring all Australians in Digital Literacy, Science, Technology, Engineering and Mathematics* is a wide ranging programme (cost at AUD 48 million) including expansion of prizes for science, development of science and mathematics resources for early education and community engagement in science.

Women and science (*Opportunities for Women in Science, Technology, Engineering and Maths*), measures include expansion of a pilot programme advocating the employment of women in science and research institutions and the promotion of female role models.

Looking forward, initiatives gearing education towards innovation should take on board the shifting consensus among experts regarding targeted support for STEM. Many countries, including Australia have for some time been endeavouring to boost student interest in STEM subjects and favouring STEM subjects in resource allocation to providers. Certainly, indicators suggest Australia scores low in terms of STEM skills. For instance, it has among the lowest share of students entering science and engineering in the OECD area. However, there is growing concern that promoting STEM may not be sufficiently fine-tuned in providing the type of skills that are likely to boost productivity and innovation in the future. The OECD's *Innovation Imperative* report (OECD, 2015b) underscores a need for policies to look beyond STEM subjects in generating innovation-rich skill sets. For instance, some categories of arts subjects can be key for innovation. The Productivity Commission's report on digital disruption underscores that by no means all STEM subjects have strong labour market demand (Productivity Commission 2016b). As suggested in the Commission's report, governments could help modify policy and student choices by improving information on employment outcomes across different subjects and across providers.

Innovation-relevant skills can also be boosted via auxiliary courses. For instance, many degree-courses are structured such that students have scope to choose "minor" subjects that do not necessarily have a direct academic connection to their main degree subject. This provides an avenue for boosting certain types of innovation-related skills. For instance, in the Netherlands since 2012 nearly all Universities and Universities of Applied Sciences offer entrepreneurship units in degree courses, and since 2016 indicators for entrepreneurship education and knowledge transfer activities are used to monitor nationwide efforts and impact.

To sum up, Australia needs to fine-tune support for STEM subjects and further improve data on labour market outcomes so as to better inform policy design and education choices.

Public-services innovation has potential to boost aggregate productivity and well-being

Public services account for a substantial share of economic activity, and therefore productivity-raising innovations can make a significant contribution to the overall productivity of the economy. Furthermore, public-service innovation can deliver fiscal savings and also bring improvements to service quality that can raise wellbeing. The OECD's *The Innovation Imperative in the Public Sector* (OECD, 2015g) divides the policy agenda into four areas, "empowering the public-sector workforce", "generating and sharing innovative ideas", "working in new ways" and "innovating within rules and processes". Table 1.5 provides some examples of Australian initiatives within this framework. Overall, the authorities have a welcome degree of commitment to boosting innovation in the public sector. In particular, Australia has programmes encouraging "bottom up" innovation from staff and processes are underway that re-examine regulation with a view to encouraging innovation. In addition, efforts to improve the measurement public-service of outputs and inputs are ongoing (see Box 1.7).

Table 1.5. **Examples of public-service policy initiatives in Australia**

Channels for public-sector innovation[1]	Examples Australian initiatives
"Empowering the public-sector workforce"	The Public Sector Innovation Toolkit (run by the Department of Industry, Innovation and Science) encourages and facilitates staff proposals for innovation in public services Innovation Champions Group, a forum for senior public-service leaders to exchange ideas and collaborate on public-service innovation
"Generating and sharing innovative ideas"	Innovation Month, an annual series of events and activities relating to public-service innovation Australian Public Service (APS) Innovation Snapshot Report which disseminates information about public-service innovations Public Sector Innovation Awards which highlight and showcase innovative practices
"Working in new ways"	The NISA notably includes efforts to get SMEs more involved in providing public services via public procurement (see main text)
"Innovating within rules and processes"	A review of public-sector regulation in the context of innovation was conducted in 2010. The review confirmed that biases towards risk-aversion and conservatism in the design of regulation were unhelpful for innovation in the public sector

1. As outlined in the OECD's *The Innovation Imperative in the Public Sector* (2015)

> **Box 1.7. Efforts to improve public-service input
> and output measurement continue**
>
> As elsewhere, Australia faces challenges in measuring many public-service outputs and
> inputs. Overcoming these can help measure (and reward) productivity-improving
> innovation and it is therefore encouraging that the authorities continue to work on
> developing data. Notably, the Australian Bureau of Statistics is developing the Health
> Services Satellite Account (HSSA), with the aim of producing estimates of output for the
> health sector that are not solely based on inputs (which is the current approach). It aims to
> do this by combining administrative health-service data with existing ABS datasets. The
> final goal is to produce estimates that can be used in the main National Accounts data.

Promoting innovative funding and delivery of human services forms a key strand of
the government's innovation agenda and picks up on a theme developed in the Harper
Review on competition policy. The idea is to increase diversity, choice and competition for
the wide range of human services that are provided across all levels of government. The
remainder of this section examines three specific policy areas that can help towards this
goal: public procurement policy, access to public-data and progress in digital services.

Public procurement: policies to get SMEs more involved

Procurement is a potentially significant channel for innovation. Indeed, the OECD has
published a report looking at cross-country experiences in encouraging innovation through
this route (OECD, 2015f). In Australia, procurement contracts account for about one third of
federal-government (Figure 1.15) expenditure and about 12 % of GDP (OECD 2015h).

Ensuring strong competition for procurement contracts is a core issue for Australia.
The Harper Review on competition policy concludes that procurement processes
often unintentionally limit the number of potential bidders by being very complex. In
some areas of procurement the number of players indeed seems low. For example, a

Figure 1.15. Public procurement spending accounts for a significant share of public spending

General government procurement as share of total government expenditures, 2013

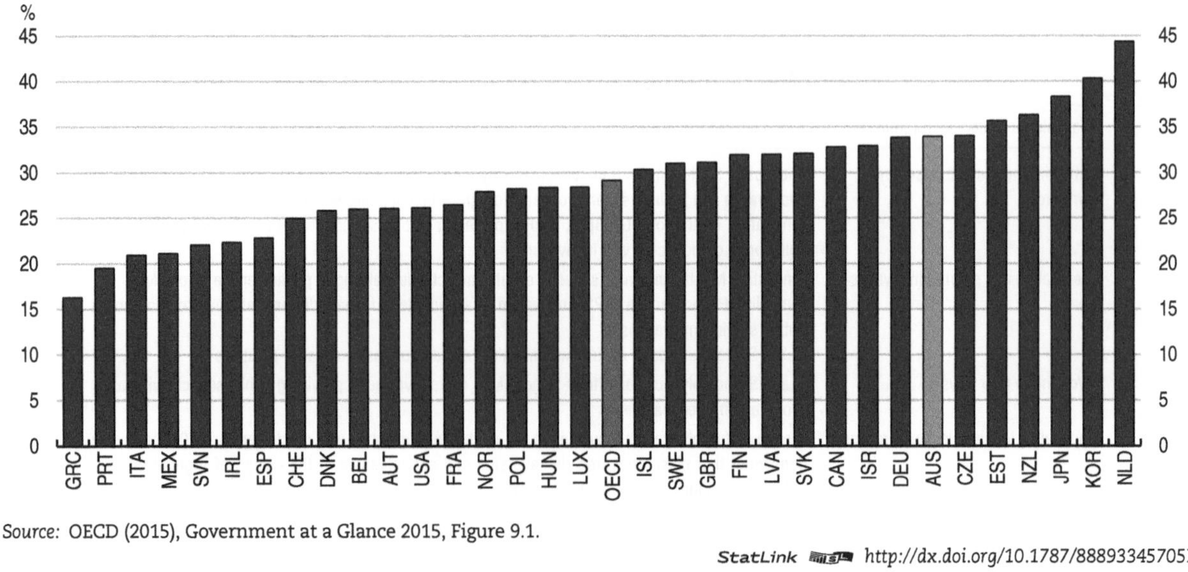

Source: OECD (2015), Government at a Glance 2015, Figure 9.1.

StatLink http://dx.doi.org/10.1787/888933457057

Productivity-Commission report on public infrastructure (Productivity Commission 2014, p. 30) discusses the apparent dominance of two company groups in large-scale public construction (in this case the Commission concluded that there is a reasonable degree of "contestability").

Recent policy initiatives promoting innovation in procurement include the following:

- "Business Research and Innovation Initiative" (launched July 2016 and part of the NISA initiative). SMEs are being invited to propose solutions to five policy and service delivery challenges with AUD 19 million earmarked for grants to develop and test the most promising ideas. Some state-level governments are already running similar programmes (for instance the *Public Sector Innovation Fund* in Victoria).

- A "digital marketplace" for information technology procurement is being established (also part of the NISA initiative). Similar to a UK programme, this will provide government agencies with an online directory of digital and technology services available from SME enterprises.

- A new procurement panel has been established by Intellectual Property Australia which provides support in cases where procurement involves IP issues, such as service delivery redesign (like shared services) or prototyping digital solutions.

These initiatives are certainly welcome, but the assessments of procurement by both the Harper Review and the Productivity Commission suggest there is plenty of scope for further action. The following avenues could be explored further:

- Widening the field of prospective bidders by decomposing procurement into smaller contracts, as intended for procurement in the ICT sector.

- Re-examination of regulatory processes for contract bidders to ensure these do not unnecessarily narrow the field. For example, the Productivity Commission specifically mentions safety accreditation processes for international prospective in the construction sector.

- Making procurement remits more conducive to innovation. One approach is to generalise the procurement remit through shifts to outcome rather than output criteria. Alternatively, tightly specified procurement contracts can be slanted to support innovation and new technologies, for instance through environmental criteria (for discussion see Edquist and Zabala-Iturriagagoitia, 2012).

- Greater efforts to inform business (especially the SME sector) about procurement opportunities and processes. Some state governments, e.g. Western Australia, already organise seminars on procurement for businesses.

Access to government data: policies aims for a more open approach

Governments collect a lot of data and there is potential for wider use for improving public services, commercial applications and general research. Australia appears to have already made good progress on this front, scoring fourth highest in an OECD indicator on the openness, usefulness and usability of government data (Figure 1.16).

A campaign is underway for government agencies to make data more widely available to business, the public at large, and other government agencies (while remaining within regulation on privacy and maintaining security features). The project employs agency-level initiative, rather than top-down directives. Finding ways of providing access to linked-up social-security, tax and company records is thought to have particularly significant potential.

Figure 1.16. **Australia has already made good progress
in making government data widely available**

Government data openness, composite index from 0 lowest to 1 highest, 2014[1]

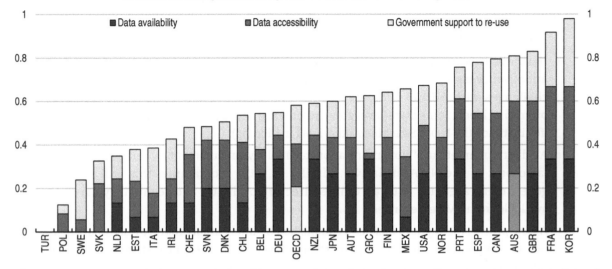

1. Responses represent countries' own assessments of current practices and procedures regarding open government data. Data refer only to central/federal governments and exclude open government data practices at the state/local levels. The composite index is based on the G8 Open Data Charter principles and on the methodology described in OECD work (Ubaldi, 2013). The OECD pilot index on Open Government Data contains 19 variables that cover information on three dimensions: i) Data availability on the national portal; ii) Data accessibility on the national portal and iii) Government support to innovative re-use of public data and stakeholder engagement. The index does not purport to measure the overall quality of the open government data approach/strategy in each country.

Source: OECD (2014), OECD Survey on Open Government Data.

StatLink ⟨ms⟩ http://dx.doi.org/10.1787/888933457065

A government report (Bureau of Communication Research, 2016) fleshes out the potential direct benefits (e.g. new products and services) and indirect benefits (e.g. greater operational efficiency in government services). The Government has also tasked the Productivity Commission to review options to improve availability and use of data, in both the public and private sector. The report is due to be delivered to the Government by 21 March 2017.

Related to this, the NISA proposes to establish a publically funded digital research unit ("Data61") by combining two current bodies, National ICT Australia Ltd (NICTA) and CSIRO's digital research unit. The aim is for the unit to help develop and apply new digital technologies (including cybersecurity research) for government and business.

Digital government services

Internet-based information and services remains an important source of innovation for governments, but also present challenges. The OECD's *Recommendation on Digital Government Strategies* provides policy guidance which underscores the need for digital government to play a more central role in in public-sector reform processes (Figure 1.17).

In general, Australia's federal and state governments have developed digital-government opportunities fairly quickly, helped by rapid adoption of internet by households and businesses. However, there is room for further progress. A consultancy report commissioned by *Adobe* (Deloitte Access Economics, 2015), estimated that out of 811 million transactions at the federal and state levels each year, about 40% still use "traditional" channels. The report estimates that a reduction to 20% could yield significant benefits to government and households with comparatively little additional outlay. Room for states to

Figure 1.17. **OECD Recommendation on Digital Government Strategies**

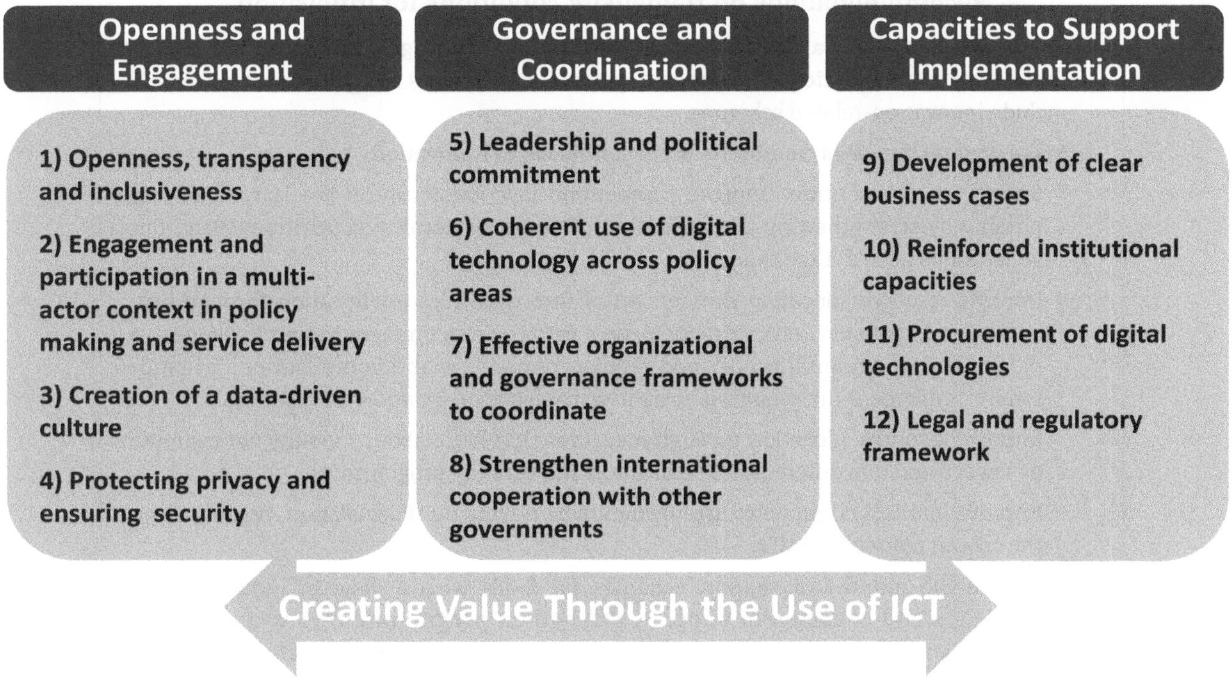

Openness and Engagement	Governance and Coordination	Capacities to Support Implementation
1) Openness, transparency and inclusiveness	5) Leadership and political commitment	9) Development of clear business cases
2) Engagement and participation in a multi-actor context in policy making and service delivery	6) Coherent use of digital technology across policy areas	10) Reinforced institutional capacities
3) Creation of a data-driven culture	7) Effective organizational and governance frameworks to coordinate	11) Procurement of digital technologies
4) Protecting privacy and ensuring security	8) Strengthen international cooperation with other governments	12) Legal and regulatory framework

Creating Value Through the Use of ICT

Source: OECD.

catch up with current best practice is part of the solution. However, the frontier of best practice in digital services is itself evolving as ICT technology and use changes, for instance enabling access to government information and services on mobile devices is now a priority.

The Deloitte study's recommendations underscore a number of themes in further developing digital government services, in particular:

● Ensuring regulation facilitates, as far as possible, digital services, including as regards privacy and security issues

● Customer focus, for example through whole-of-government portals

● Household access and awareness to digital services; bringing "offline" segments of the population on board reduces the need for parallel "traditional" services

● Transitioning government services and staff in the wake of digitisation. Maximising the returns to digitisation often requires significant change in staffing requirements

The Australian authorities are focussing on a number of these issues. The federal government established the Digital Transformation Office (DTO) in 2015, which is charged with making public services simpler, faster and more convenient. The aim is to make services digital by design, rather than bolting on digital services to existing systems. It was renamed the Digital Transformation Agency (DTA) in October 2016, with an expanded remit that includes ICT procurement policy.

Summing up the policy challenges in public-sector innovation

Australia needs to continue encouraging innovation in public services, in particular by widening the field for procurement applications, shifts towards outcome rather than output criteria in contracting and greater accessibility and usefulness of public-sector data. Continued efforts to develop digital government services are required.

Recommendations on framework conditions for innovation

- **Ensure productivity is a core focus of innovation policy alongside focus on innovation that benefits wider society**. The support system for Australia's indigenous people should include innovation-related schemes.

- **Make general business conditions more conducive to innovation:**

  - ❖ Strengthen competition. Improve competition law, follow up on the Harper Review, notably by strengthening the definition of abuse of dominant position. Weed out superfluous good's standards.

  - ❖ Improve resource allocation through better firm dynamics (reallocation through firm entry, exit, expansion and contraction): deal with the remaining red-tape challenges, in particular implementation of good regulatory practice and complications in land-tenure, implement the proposals to lighten insolvency regulation for creditors.

  - ❖ Improve resource allocation through measures that help labour mobility, for example by lower interstate differences in education and training programmes.

  - ❖ Improve intellectual property arrangements by tidying up IP legislation, notably scrap the special regime for SMEs.

  - ❖ Reduce the number of support schemes for SMEs with a view to increasing the efficiency and cohesion of support. Strengthen programme review and reform mechanisms, taking into account the risk that support can discourage firms' expansion. Ensure awareness of schemes by firms.

- **Encourage market entry by innovative business ("disruptors") while also checking for downsides:**

  - ❖ Use competition-policy tools to combat resistance by incumbents and ensure fair treatment between incumbents and disruptors in the tax system and in business support mechanisms.

  - ❖ Adjust sectoral regulation quickly as new business models and services emerge.

  - ❖ In personal transport, in the long run aim for no regulatory distinction between taxis and new forms of service. In accommodation services, set up processes to identify the most effective regulatory approaches across local governments and encourage convergence to them.

- **Improve ICT** for Australian households and businesses. In mobile telephony, facilitate the entry of a fourth operator and continue work on solutions to rural coverage (for instance by using towers being installed for broadband). In fixed-line technology encourage the wholesaler (NBN) to give greater technical and pricing flexibility to retailers.

- In **education policy** widen the scope of subsidies for innovation-related subjects beyond STEM to include other subjects such as innovation-related arts disciplines.

- Continue to **encourage innovation in public services** by opening up procurement to a wider range of bidders, through shifts towards outcome rather than output criteria in contracting and through increasing the accessibility and usefulness of public-sector data. Continue to develop digital government services.

Bibliography

Aghion, P., S. Bechtold, L. Cassar, H. Herz (2014), "Causal effects of competition on innovation: experimental evidence", *National Bureau of Economic Research*, Working Paper 19987.

Banks, G. (2010), *An Economy-wide View: Speeches on Structural Reform*, Productivity Commission, March 2010.

Bureau of Communications Research (2016), *Open government data and why it matters*, Commonwealth of Australia, 2016.

De Steel, A. and P. Larouche (2015), *Disruptive Innovation and Competition Policy Enforcement*, OECD Global Forum on Competition, October 2015.

Deloitte Access Economics (2015), *Digital government transformation*, 2015, commissioned by Adobe, 2015.

Deloitte Access Economics (2016), *Economic effects of ridesharing in Australia. A report prepared for Uber*, 2016.

Edquist C. and J.M. Zabala-Iturriagagoitia (2012), "Public Procurement for Innovation as mission-oriented innovation policy", *Research Policy*, 41 (2012).

Égert, B. (2016), *Regulation, Institutions, and Productivity: New Macroeconomic Evidence from OECD Countries*, American Economic Review, 106(5): 109-13.

Eslake (2011), *Productivity: the lost decade*, paper presented to the annual policy conference of the Reserve Bank of Australia, August, 2011.

Government of Australia (2015), *Regional Telecommunications Review 2015*, Canberra, 2015.

Government of Australia (2016), *Improving bankruptcy and insolvency laws: proposals paper*, April 2016.

Guellec, D. and van Pottelsberghe de la Potterie, B. (2001), *R&D and productivity growth: panel data analysis of 16 OECD countries*, OECD Economic Studies No. 33, 2001/II.

Harper, I., P. Anderson, S. McCluskey, M. O'Bryan QC (2015b), *Competition Policy Review, Final Report*, Commonwealth of Australia, March.

Khan, M. et al. (2010), *How robust is the R&D – productivity relationship? Evidence from OECD countries*, WIPO Economic Research Working Papers No. 1, December 2010.

KPMG (2016), *Harnessing Potential: Asia-Pacific Alternative Finance Benchmarking Report*, March 2016.

McGowan, M.A. and D. Andrews, (2015), *Skill Mismatch and Public Policy in OECD Countries*, OECD Economics Department Working Papers, No. 1210.

McGowan, M.A, and D. Andrews (2016), "Insolvency regimes and productivity growth: a framework for analysis", *Economics Department Working Paper Series* No. 1309.

Minifie, J. (2016), *Peer-to-peer pressure, Policy for the sharing economy*, Grattan Institute, 2016.

OECD (2014a), *Productivity Growth and Innovation in the Long Run, Proceedings*, Joint OECD-NBER Conference Paris 25-26 September 2014, OECD Publishing, Paris.

OECD (2014b), "Wireless Market Structures and Network Sharing", OECD *Digital Economy Papers*, No. 243, 2014.

OECD (2015a), *The Future of Productivity*, OECD Publishing, Paris.

OECD (2015b), *The Innovation Imperative*, OECD Publishing Paris.

OECD (2015c), *Innovation Policies for Inclusive Growth*, OECD Publishing Paris.

OECD (2015d), *Hearing on Disruptive Innovation*, Issues paper by the Secretariat, June 2015, OECD.

OECD (2015e), *Hearing on Disruptive Innovation in the financial sector*, Note by the Secretariat, October 2015, OECD.

OECD (2015f), *Digital Economy Outlook*, OECD Publishing, Paris.

OECD (2015g), *The Innovation Imperative in the Public Sector*, OECD Publishing, Paris.

OECD, (2015h), Government at a Glance 2015, OECD Publishing, Paris.

OECD (2016a), "No Country for Young Firms? Start-up Dynamics and National Policies", OECD *Science, Technology and Industry Policy Papers*, No. 29.

OECD (2016b), *Protecting and Promoting Competition in Response to "Disruptive" Innovations in Legal Services,* Note by the Secretariat, June 2016, OECD.

Productivity Commission (2015), *Business Set-up, Transfer and Closure,* Productivity Commission Inquiry Report, No. 75, 30.

Productivity Commission (2016a), *Intellectual Property Arrangements,* Productivity Commission Draft Report, April 2016.

Productivity Commission (2016b), *Digital Disruption, What do governments need to do?* Productivity Commission Research Paper, June 2016.

Saia, A. , D. Andrews and S. Abrizio (2015), "Productivity Spillovers from the Global Frontier and public Policy", OECD *Economic Department Working Papers,* No, 1238.

Shanks, S. and Zheng, S. (2006), *Econometric Modelling of R&D and Australia's Productivity,* Productivity Commission Staff Working Paper, Canberra, April 2006.

Chapter 2

Boosting R&D outcomes

> R&D activity can play a central role in raising productivity. Australia compares well in terms of research excellence. However, there is scope for better translation of publicly funded research into commercial outcomes. Strengthening incentives for collaborative research is essential. A simpler funding system for university research that provides sharper and more transparent incentives for research partnerships is important in this regard. Research-business linkages would also be boosted by more effective programmes encouraging business to collaborate, measures promoting greater mobility of researchers between the two sectors, and steps to ensure that intellectual property arrangements are not a barrier to knowledge. In Australia financial support for encouraging business innovation relies mostly on an R&D tax incentive; raising additionality and reducing compliance costs would enhance the effectiveness of the scheme. Maximising the benefits from public investment in research further hinges upon a well-coordinated science, research and innovation system through a "whole-of-government" approach and consolidating certain programmes. Reform initiatives underway, notably those in the National Innovation and Science Agenda, are welcome.

The statistical data for Israel are supplied by and under the responsibility of the relevant Israeli authorities. The use of such data by the OECD is without prejudice to the status of the Golan Heights, East Jerusalem and Israeli settlements in the West Bank under the terms of international law.

Innovation input is stronger than output

Australia can make more out of its R&D spending

Australia is well above the OECD median in terms of overall innovation "input", according to the *2016 Global Innovation Index* (Figure 2.1), reflecting a well-developed research system (Box 2.1), a strong skill base and a supportive institutional framework. Measures of research excellence, such as publications in top international scientific journals and citations, reveal a healthy "academic impact" (Figure 2.3, Panels A to C). Furthermore, six Australian universities rank among the top 100 on the basis of research-related indicators (Figure 2.3, Panel D).

Gross expenditure on R&D (GERD) as a percentage of GDP in Australia is middle-ranking (Figure 2.4, Panel A). This measure of R&D intensity grew rapidly between 2000 and 2008, catching up with the OECD average (weighted), but has fallen in recent years (Figure 2.4, Panels B and C). This decline mainly reflects trends in the business sector, and in particular a slowdown in mining-related R&D associated with the end of commodity-sector boom (Figure 2.4 and Box 2.2). The higher education sector has contributed positively with its share in total R&D exceeding the OECD average in 2013 (Figure 2.4, Panels C and D). The share of the government-performed R&D fell somewhat between 2000 and 2013; however, this only partially reflects the government's role as it supports R&D in universities and businesses via grants and tax incentives (Figure 2.6).

Figure 2.1. **There is scope to better match innovation input and output**

Global Innovation Index: input-output matrix, 2016[1]

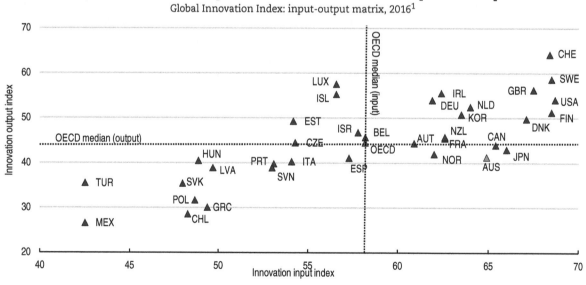

1. Innovation input measures include: institutions, human capital and research, infrastructure, market and business sophistication. Output measures include: knowledge and technology outputs and creative outputs. The indicators were normalised into the [0,100] range, with higher scores representing better outcomes.

Source: Cornell University, INSEAD, and WIPO (2016): The Global Innovation Index 2016: Winning with Global Innovation.

StatLink ▉▉▉ *http://dx.doi.org/10.1787/888933457073*

Box 2.1. **Australia's research system**

Australia's research system consists of universities, public-sector research agencies (PSRAs), businesses, and also an array of smaller organisations and structures (Australian Universities, 2014). In particular:

- There are currently 41 universities (3 of which are private). Higher education absorbs the largest share of Commonwealth support for science and innovation (34% of total in 2016-17) (Figure 2.2). University research is supported through a "dual" federal funding system of competitive grants and Research Block Grants (RBG) (discussed further below). The competitive grant component is made up of merit-based, peer-reviewed programmes, administrated mainly by the *Australian Research Council* (ARC) and *National Health and Medical Research Council* (NHMRC) (Watt, 2015a,b). These competitive programmes only cover the direct costs of the research projects. RBG are not tied to specific projects and support the indirect costs (e.g. overheads, facilities and equipment) of competitive grant-funded research.

- Australia's most prominent public-sector research agency (PSRA) is the Commonwealth Scientific and Industrial Research Organisation (CSIRO) (discussed further below). Other agencies include, for instance: the Defence Science and Technology Organisation (DSTO), Australian Nuclear Science and Technology Organisation (ANTO), Geoscience Australia, and Australian Institute of Marine Science (AIMS).

- Australia's research system also includes other organisations and structures. The *Cooperative Research Centres* (CRC) programme, for instance, supports end-user driven collaboration among publicly funded researchers, business and the community. The number of CRC programmes has fallen in recent years (there were 33 programmes in 2015-16, compared with 70 in 2006). There are also 15 *Rural Research and Development Corporations* (RDCs) that fund government-industry research projects. Moreover, there are many non-profit research institutes, for instance, over 60 in medical research (Australian Universities, 2014).

Figure 2.2. **Australian Government support for science, research and innovation by sector, 2016-17**

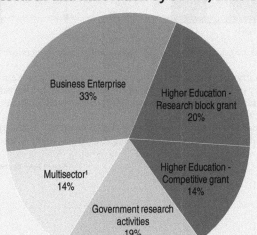

1. Multisector includes R&D expenditure on activities that may be undertaken within more than one of the other sectors (e.g. NHMRC grants are available to universities but also to medical research institutes, government bodies and hospitals).

Source: Australian Department of Industry, Innovation and Science (2016), The Australian Government's 2016-17 Science, Research and Innovation Budget Tables.

StatLink ᴍᵟᴇᴘ *http://dx.doi.org/10.1787/888933457088*

Figure 2.3. **Research quality compares well internationally**

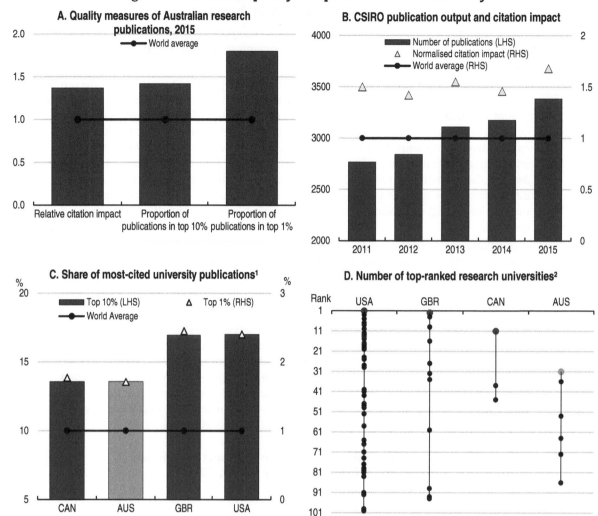

1. Data are based on publications produced during 2011-14. For each country, only universities with at least 5000 publucations during the period are considered.
2. Number of universities in each country that are ranked in the top 100 of Times Higher Education (THE) World University Rankings 2015-16. The ranking of each country is depicted on a line connecting the highest and lowest ranked ones among the world top 100 universities. The research score is calculated as a weighted average of three relevant indicators: research reputation (60%), research income (20%) and research productivity (20%).

Source: Australian Department of Industry, Innovation and Science (2016), Australian Innovation System Report 2016; CSIRO (2016), Annual Report 2015–16; Leiden University (2016), CWTS Leiden Ranking 2016; Times Higher Education (2016), World University Rankings 2015-2016.

StatLink ▉▉▉ *http://dx.doi.org/10.1787/888933457095*

Figure 2.4. **R&D trends and international comparisons**

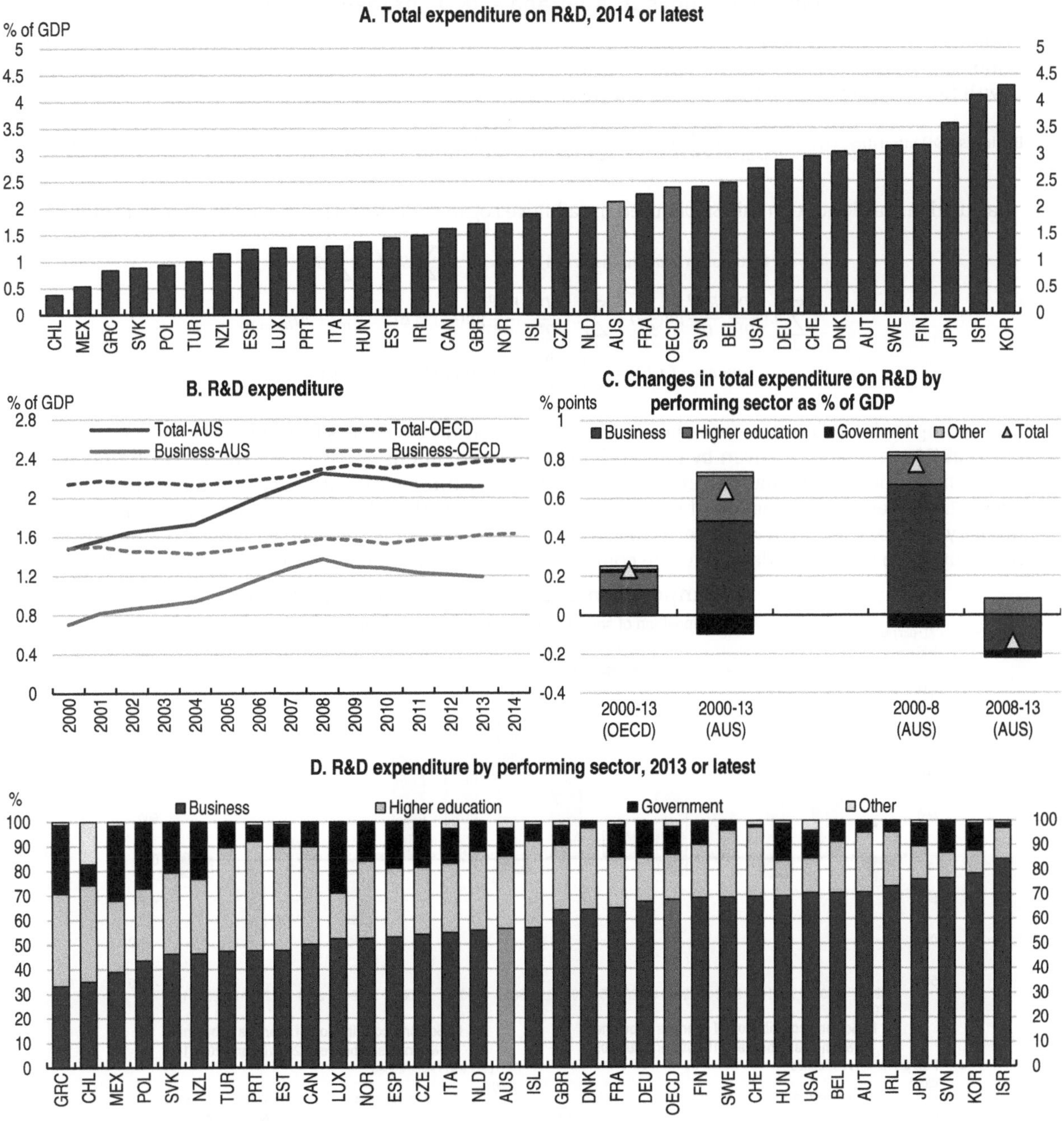

A. Total expenditure on R&D, 2014 or latest

B. R&D expenditure

C. Changes in total expenditure on R&D by performing sector as % of GDP

D. R&D expenditure by performing sector, 2013 or latest

Source: OECD (2016), OECD Main Science and Technology Indicators (database).

StatLink ᵃᵃˢᵇ http://dx.doi.org/10.1787/888933457102

Box 2.2. **Explaining changes in Australia's R&D, intensity versus composition**

Changes in economy-wide R&D intensity can arise from changing intensities within sectors of the economy but also from changes in industry composition (i.e. structure effects), for example, through rapid growth in R&D-intensive sectors such as pharmaceuticals and ICT equipment. More formally:

$$\text{Business R\&D intensity } (I) = \frac{Business\ R\&D\ (RD)}{Business\ VA\ (Q)} = \sum_{i=sector} \frac{Q_i}{Q}\frac{RD_i}{Q_i} = \sum_i S_i I_i = \text{Structure effect} \times \text{Within} - \text{sector Intensity effect}$$

Calculations carried out for this *Survey* used the additive Logarithmic Mean Divisia Index method (Ang, 2004):

$$\text{Changes in total intensity } (\Delta I) = I^T - I^0 = \sum_i S_i^T I_i^T - \sum_i S_i^0 I_i^0$$

$$= \sum_i L\left(\frac{RD_i^T}{Q^T}, \frac{RD_i^0}{Q^0}\right)\ln\left(\frac{S_i^T}{S_i^0}\right) + \sum_i L\left(\frac{RD_i^T}{Q^T}, \frac{RD_i^0}{Q^0}\right)\ln\left(\frac{I_i^T}{I_i^0}\right) = \Delta I_{structure} + \Delta I_{Intensity}$$

$$\text{where } L(a,b) = \frac{a-b}{(lna - lnb)} \ (i.e.\ logarithmic\ mean)$$

According to the results, the continuous increases in Australia's business R&D intensity between 2000/01 and 2008/09 were largely driven by growth in within-sector intensity. However, the intensity has been falling since the global financial crisis, through both within-sector intensity and structural effects. (Figure 2.5, Panel A). Examination of specific industries reveals that the post-global financial crisis fall in intensity is mainly due to developments in R&D investment in mining, especially in metal ore mining, and lower output share of manufacturing, the country's most R&D intensive sector (Figure 2.5, Panels B and C).

Figure 2.5. **Decomposition analysis on business R&D intensity**

A. Decomposition of annual changes in business R&D intensity

B. Sectoral contribution of changes in business R&D intensity between 1999/00 and 2008/09

C. Sectoral contribution of changes in business R&D intensity between 2008/09 and 2013/14

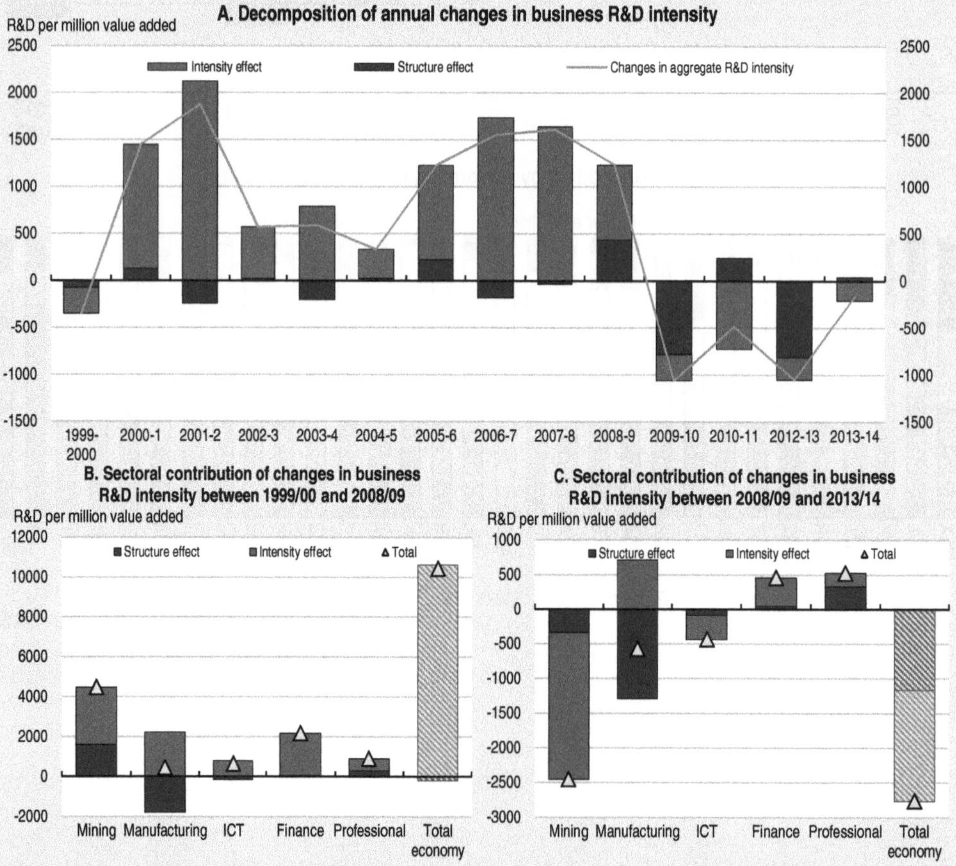

Source: OECD calculations based on ABS (2015), 8104.0 – Research and Experimental Development, Businesses and 5204.0 – Australian System of National Accounts, 2015-16.

StatLink ⟨⟩ http://dx.doi.org/10.1787/888933457117

Figure 2.6. **R&D expenditure by source of funding**

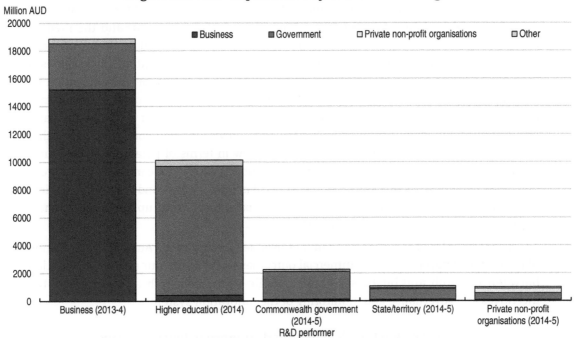

Source: ABS, 8104.0 – Research and Experimental Development, Businesses, Australia, 2013-14; 8109.0 – Research and Experimental Development, Government and Private Non-Profit Organisatiàons, Australia, 2014-15; 8111.0 – Research and Experimental Development, Higher Education Organisations, Australia, 2014. *StatLink* ⬛⬛ *http://dx.doi.org/10.1787/888933457127*

Figure 2.7. **Some critical innovation outcomes are low in international comparison**

Innovation output indicators[1]

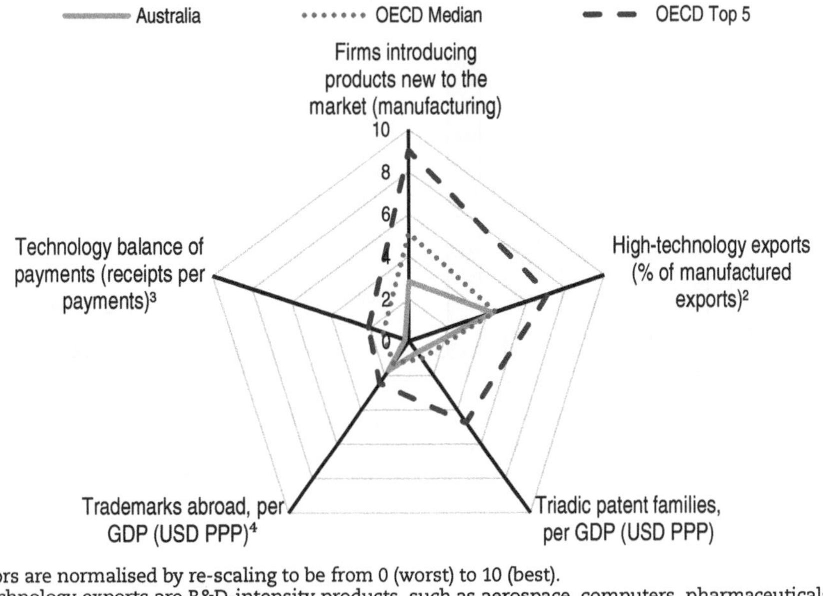

—— Australia   •••••• OECD Median   – – OECD Top 5

Firms introducing products new to the market (manufacturing)

High-technology exports (% of manufactured exports)[2]

Technology balance of payments (receipts per payments)[3]

Triadic patent families, per GDP (USD PPP)

Trademarks abroad, per GDP (USD PPP)[4]

1. Indicators are normalised by re-scaling to be from 0 (worst) to 10 (best).
2. High-technology exports are R&D-intensity products, such as aerospace, computers, pharmaceuticals, scientific instruments, and electrical machinery.
3. This measure consists of money paid, or received, for the use of IP and technical services (including technical assistance) and for industrial R&D carried out abroad, etc.
4. Trademarks abroad correspond to the number of applications filed at the United States, EU and Japan, by application date and country of residence of the applicant. For the United States, EU members and Japan, counts exclude applications in their domestic market. Counts are rescaled by taking into account the relative average propensity of other countries to file in these three offices.

Source: OECD (2015), OECD Science, Technology and Industry Scoreboard 2015; World Bank (2016), World Development Indicators (database); OECD (2014), OECD Science, Technology and Industry Outlook 2014; OECD, Main Science and Technology Indicators (database). *StatLink* ⬛⬛ *http://dx.doi.org/10.1787/888933457132*

While the inputs of Australia's innovation system rank high among OECD countries, output indicators are less impressive. Innovation output is, of course, difficult to measure. According to the *Global Innovation Index*, Australia's output is only around the median (Figure 2.1), and specific indicators, such as triadic patents and "new-to-market" innovations, compare unfavourably internationally (Figure 2.7). To an extent, the low rates of "creative" innovation can be explained by the importance of "imported" innovation in Australia (Chapter 1). The large weight of the mining sector in the Australian economy may be an additional reason for the relatively weak innovation outcomes as the sector has a comparatively low patent intensity (OFHIM, 2013). However, even compared with other advanced resource-rich countries, Australia ranks low in terms of patent-based measures (Figure 2.8). It also performs poorly in translating publicly funded research into commercial outcomes. Patenting revenue and other measures of knowledge flow and commercialisation, including the impact of publicly funded research on patents and start-up companies formed, lag behind those in OECD peers (Figure 2.9).

The remainder of this chapter examines avenues for improving Australia's translation of its research knowledge into commercial outcomes focusing on four areas: collaboration between research and business sectors, public-sector research agencies, R&D tax incentives and governance and monitoring of the innovation system.

Figure 2.8. **Australia's patent performance is below average**
Patent intensity, 2013

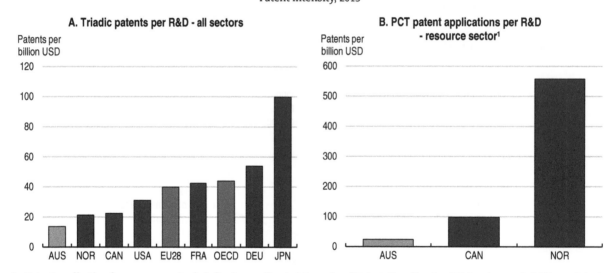

1. Patent application for resource sector is defined according to International Patent Classification E21 (earth or rock drilling; mining).
Source: OECD (2016), OECD Main Science and Technology Indicators.

StatLink ⬛ *http://dx.doi.org/10.1787/888933457142*

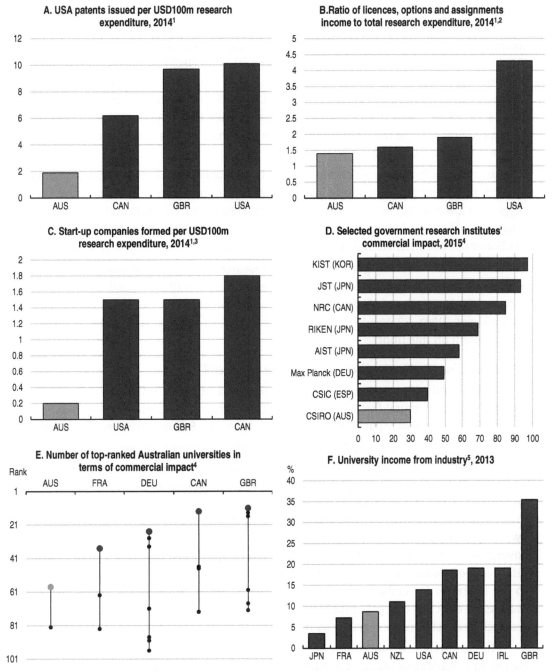

Figure 2.9. **Commercialisation outcomes are lagging behind**

1. Data for publicly funded research organisations, which include universities, publicly funded research agencies and medical research institutes.
2. A licence agreement formalises the transfer of technology between two parties. An option agreement grants the potential licensee a period to evaluate the technology and negotiate a licence agreement. An assignment agreement conveys all rights, titles and interests in the licenced subject matter to the named assignee.
3. Start-up companies that are partially or entirely dependent on the licensing or assignment of an institution's technology for initiation.
4. "Commercial impact" indicates how often basic research originating at an institution has influenced commercial R&D activity, as measured by academic papers cited in patent filings. The selection of institutes is based on comparable annual budget size.
5. Includes funds from business enterprises, private non-profit and abroad.

Source: Australian Department of Industry, Innovation and Science (2016), National Survey of Research Commercialisation (NSRC); Reuters (2016), Top 25 Global Innovators – Government; Scimago Lab (2016), Scimago Institutions Rankings; OECD (2015), OECD Science, Technology and Industry Scoreboard 2015.

StatLink http://dx.doi.org/10.1787/888933457151

Weak collaboration between research and business sectors remains a key issue

Australia's difficulty in commercialising publicly funded research reflects a low level of collaborative research, which is an increasingly recognised channel of knowledge transfer (OECD, 2013; OECD, 2015a). Australia ranks last among 26 OECD countries with respect to the proportion of businesses collaborating with higher education or public-sector research agencies on innovation (Figure 2.10, Panel A). Only 3% of Australian innovation-active firms source their ideas from the research sector, while 60% of ideas come from sources within the firm, though the results vary somewhat across sectors and with the size of firm (Figure 2.10, Panels B and C).

Australia also has a low incidence of co-authored publications between industry and the research sector and a comparatively low concentration of researchers in the business sector, suggesting low mobility between the two sectors (Figure 2.10, Panels D and E). Evidence on international linkages is more mixed: co-operation on publications and patenting is below the OECD average, but international mobility of scientific authors is relatively high (Figure 2.11).

There are undoubtedly good examples of research-industry collaboration in Australia such as the Cooperative Research Centre for Green House Gas (Box 2.3) and the partnership between the University of New South Wales and Onesteel for the development of specific technologies (Watt, 2015a). However, it is clear that, in broad terms, there is room for improvement on this front.

What explains the low level of collaborative research?

Differing priorities and cultures of universities and firms, reflecting differences in objectives, and structural factors, such as the importance of "imported" innovation, partly explain the low level of collaboration (PwC et al., 2015; The Senate, 2015; Ferris et al., 2016).

As highlighted in the 2012 Survey (OECD, 2012), one specific driver of Australia's low level of collaborative research is that the tight linkage between promotion opportunities and publication outcomes in higher education is likely reducing researchers' incentives to engage with industry. Universities place a high value on research excellence, as this is key in determining their international ranking and reputation (Australian Government, 2014a; PwC et al., 2015). Moreover, research excellence is important in determining federal-government transfers to universities (though its importance has fallen under current reforms, see below). Long administrative procedures for competitive grants (see below) add to the obstacles for collaborative research. Furthermore, a recent review stressed the dissuasive effect of charges imposed by university administrations on commissioned research or consultancy, especially as regards small-scale projects (The Senate, 2015).

The relatively low proportion of researchers employed in industry can be another barrier to collaborative research (Figure 2.10, Panel E). This is reflected in the early career paths of research graduates. For example, survey data show that in 2012 only a quarter of Masters/PhD graduates were working in the private sector in that year (Australian Government, 2014b). The relatively limited in scale and scope industry placement programmes and low levels of mobility between research and business sectors explain, to a large extent, these patterns (PwC et al., 2015; McGagh, 2016). Both universities and industry need to be more open to collaborative opportunities and to sharing expertise. A recent government report on the innovation system highlights the importance of the science and research skills that are found in academia and public research organisations for "new-to-market" innovations (Australian Government, 2014c).

Figure 2.10. **Collaborative research in limited**

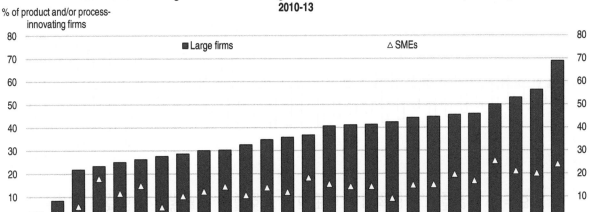

A. Firms collaborating on innovation with higher education or research institutions by firm size, 2010-13

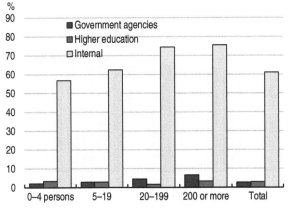

B. Sources of ideas or information for business innovation by employment size, 2014-15

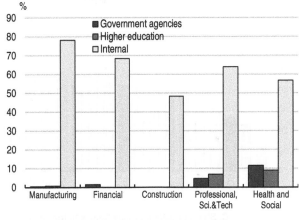

C. Sources of ideas or information for business innovation by industry, 2014-15

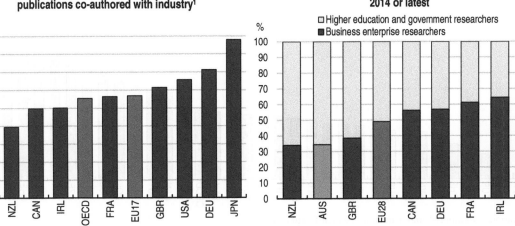

D. Proportion of higher education research publications co-authored with industry[1]

E. Share of researchers by performing sector, 2014 or latest

1. Includes universities having produced more than 5000 publications during 2010-13.
Source: OECD (2014, 2015), OECD Science, Technology and Industry Scoreboard; Australian Department of Industry, Innovation and Science (2016), Australian Innovation System Report; ABS, 8158.0 – Innovation in Australian Business, 2014-15; Leiden University (2016), CWTS Leiden Ranking 2016; OECD (2015), Main Science and Technology Indicators: Volume 2015/2.

StatLink http://dx.doi.org/10.1787/888933457166

Figure 2.11. **International collaboration performance is mixed**

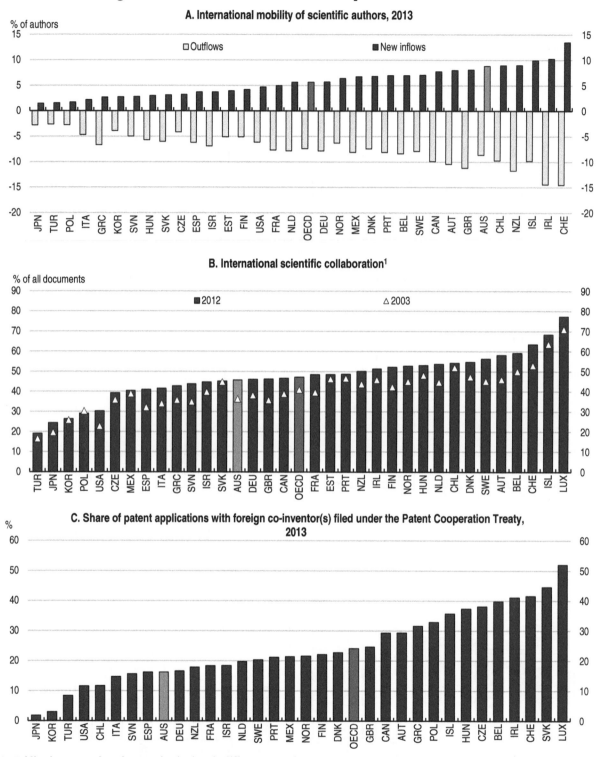

A. International mobility of scientific authors, 2013

B. International scientific collaboration[1]

C. Share of patent applications with foreign co-inventor(s) filed under the Patent Cooperation Treaty, 2013

1. Publications co-authored among institutions in different countries.

Source: OECD (2015), OECD Science, Technology and Industry Scoreboard 2015; OECD (2016), OECD Patent Statistics (database).

StatLink ⟨≡⟩ http://dx.doi.org/10.1787/888933457178

Box 2.3. **Australia's Cooperative Research Centres programme:
an example of strong collaborative research**

Since the *Cooperative Research Centres programme* (Box 2.1) began in the early 1990s, government has provided over AUD 4 billion in support and other stakeholders have contributed a further AUD 12.3 billion (Australian Government, 2016a). It is estimated the economy-wide benefit has been more than triple the value of government support, adding about 0.03 percentage points to annual GDP growth (Allen Consulting Group, 2012). Government spending on the programme has been reduced to 1.5% of total government support for science, research and innovation in 2015-6, from its peak level of 3.9% in 1997-8 (Figure 2.12, Panel A).

Cooperative Research Centre for Greenhouse Gas Technologies (CO2CRC) – Green innovation

The CO2CRC is a Centre based in the University of Melbourne, which specialises in research on Carbon Capture and Storage (CCS). After 11 years of funding CO2CRC exited the program in 2014 and continues to operate with the support of other programmes including the Government CCS Flagships Program (*CarbonNet project*), funded by the Education Investment Fund (CO2CRC, 2015).

CO2CRC has successfully developed the country's first deep geological CO_2 storage process (*Otway Project*). The Project completed end-to-end demonstration of CCS technologies on the largest scale globally to date. It has provided valuable new data for the development of government policy and global energy market development (State Government of Victoria, 2016).

A key feature of CO2CRC is its extensive collaboration of industry, research organisations, government and international partners. As of 2013-14, 33 domestic and foreign organisations were participating in the Centre either through providing staff or funding. This diverse base of support is a key factor to the success of the Centre (Figure 2.12, Panel B).

Figure 2.12. **Trends in CRC and funding composition of CO2CRC**

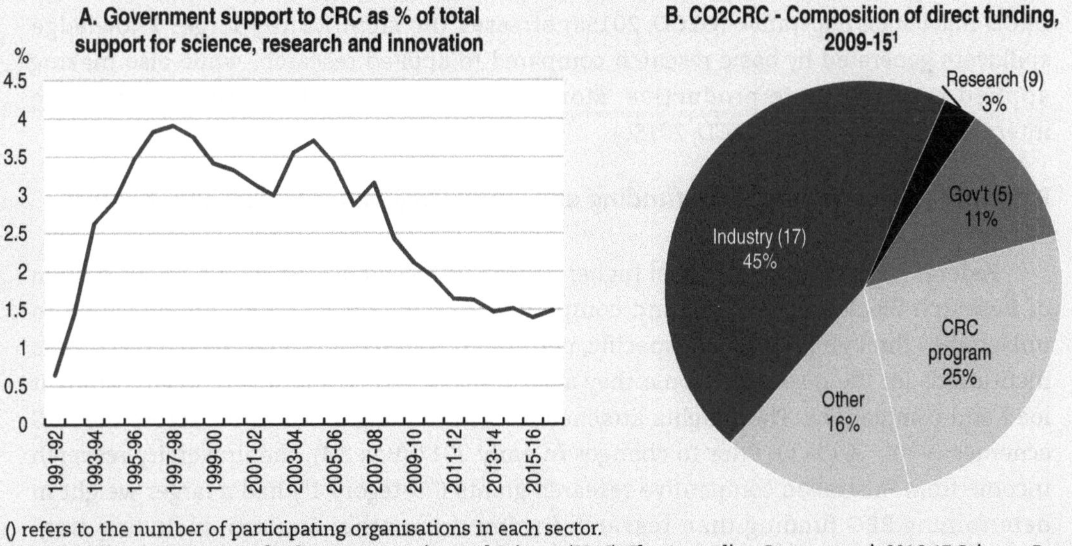

A. Government support to CRC as % of total support for science, research and innovation

B. CO2CRC - Composition of direct funding, 2009-15[1]

Research (9) 3%
Gov't (5) 11%
Industry (17) 45%
CRC program 25%
Other 16%

1. () refers to the number of participating organisations in each sector.
Source: Australian Department of Industry, Innovation and Science (2016), The Australian Government's 2016-17 Science, Research and Innovation Budget Tables; CO2CRC (2015), Annual Report 2014.

StatLink ⬛ http://dx.doi.org/10.1787/888933457189

The universities' systems for managing intellectual property (IP) are also potentially problematic for industry-university collaboration and knowledge diffusion. The Productivity Commission highlighted, for instance, dissuasive transaction costs, especially for small and medium-sized enterprises (SMEs), in accessing university IP due to the large variety of IP arrangements across universities (and often within them too) (PC, 2007). An inquiry in 2012 concluded that delays in IP negotiations are a "major obstacle" to collaboration between industry and publicly funded research organisations (ACIP, 2012). According to this report, it takes typically 10 months to negotiate IP contracts, with delays commonly relating to agreement over the ownership of IP created in the process of collaboration, publication rights and accurate valuation of the IP. Furthermore, a recent review of university research funding (discussed below) highlights concerns raised by industry groups about overvaluation of IP by some universities and shortages of academic staff with sufficient prior commercialisation experience (Watt, 2015b). A lack of clarity on IP ownership for students on industry placements is seen by industry groups as a further obstacle to collaboration.

Policy levers for strengthening collaboration between the research and business sectors

Boosting collaborative research is closely related to encouraging universities and business to engage, with research funding arrangements and business-focused collaboration programmes being obvious levers. Effective management of IP created by university research and increased mobility between research and business sectors are also important for enhancing knowledge flow. All these areas are discussed below.

Strengthening collaboration does not imply a need for reduced attention to basic research. Indeed, there are good reasons for continuing support for such research. The *OECD Innovation Imperative* (OECD, 2015a) stresses the significantly larger knowledge spillovers generated by basic research compared to applied research, while also making applied research more productive. Moreover, basic research facilitates access to international knowledge (OECD, 2015b).

Reforming university research funding and monitoring better the broader benefits of research

Federal-government funding of higher education research comprises a "dual" system of Research Block Grants (RBG) and competitive grants (Box 2.1). RBG are allocated to universities through programme-specific, performance-based formulae, which reward the institutions for the research income they attract, publications, and higher degree student load and completions. The weights attached to each funding driver differ across the RBG schemes (Watt, 2015a,b). Prior to changes in early 2017 (Box 2.4), the university research income from Australian competitive research grants ("Category 1") had a larger weight in determining RBG funding than research income from other sources, including from industry ("Category 2-4").

The RBG cover a relatively small proportion of total university research expenditure, around 16% in 2014 (Figure 2.13). Other sources, notably "general university funds", which include Commonwealth funding not specifically targeted at research, play a greater role. But RBG account for a large proportion of government support under the dual funding system for university research. In addition, they entail schemes that support the indirect costs of research, research training, as well as collaborative efforts (Watt, 2015 a,b).

Box 2.4. **The main features of the reform of the higher education research arrangements**

A government-commissioned review on research policy and funding of higher education (Watt Review) in 2015 identified several avenues to increase the returns from public investment in universities (Watt, 2015b). The review notably recommended a new funding system for university research that is less complex and provides greater incentives for collaboration and research commercialisation. It also recommended a comprehensive approach to assessing the wider benefits of publicly funded research. Reforms are underway in response to the review's recommendations. In particular:

Research funding arrangements

- A new model for Research Block Grants (RBG), announced as part of the recent *National Innovation and Science Agenda* (NISA), began operating in early 2017. The new arrangements are combining the six existing RBG schemes into two: a *Research Support Programme* (RSP) and a *Research Training Programme* (RTP). Block grants for the RSP are now allocated exclusively on the basis of research income, with an increase in the weight attached to the income from business and other end-users ("Category 2-4"). This income category is now given equal weight to income from Australian competitive grants ("Category 1") (Watt, 2015b; Williams, 2016). This means that publications and higher degree student load no longer feature in the RSP funding formulae (Australian Government, 2016b). Publications are also removed from the RPT funding formulae. Student completions and research income across Categories 1-4 are retained as drivers for research training funding, each with equal weight.

- In addition, changes to the competitive grant programmes are underway, aiming to increase their responsiveness to applicants' needs and boost collaborative research. Notably, the *Australian Research Council (ARC) Linkage Projects* – designed to support research partnerships between universities and businesses and other end-users – have moved to a continuous application and assessment process (rather than one round per year as was previously the case), accompanied by a fast-track decision-making process; grant decisions were taking up to 9 months under the annual selection process (Watt, 2015b). In addition, measures will be taken to facilitate assessment and prioritisation of proposals with commercialisation and business collaboration potential.

Impact assessment

- A new framework for assessing the "impact" of university research is being developed (Australian Government, 2016b). Currently, the quality of university research is gauged by the *Excellence in Research for Australia* (ERA) – a national evaluation framework (Australian Government, 2011). ERA is based on expert review informed by a range of indicators including citation profiles and peer review of a sample of research outputs. The ratings against national and international benchmarks are determined by committees of researchers, drawn from Australia and overseas (ARC, 2016). The framework under development intends to compliment the ERA with new measures – qualitative and quantitative – that enable assessment of university research performance in terms of non-academic impact and end-user engagement (Australian Government, 2015a; 2016b). The government plans to implement the new framework in 2018, following a pilot project in 2017.

Figure 2.13. **Higher education R&D expenditure by source of funding, 2014**

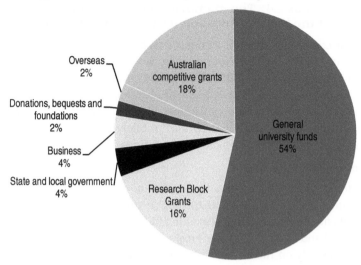

Source: ABS (2016), 8111.0 – Research and Experimental Development, Higher Education Organisations, Australia, 2014.

StatLink ᴍᴍᴵᴳᴵᴸ *http://dx.doi.org/10.1787/888933457192*

However, the Research Block Grant system has been judged as "unnecessarily complex", and as failing to provide clear incentives regarding collaboration with business and other end-users (Watt, 2015b).

The reforms underway to the funding system for university research (Box 2.4) go in the right direction and should be implemented as envisaged. A simpler allocation formula for block funding, along with a more balanced weighting between the role of university research income from competitive grants and income from other sources (mainly business), provide sharper and more transparent incentives for collaborative research. Changes in the competitive grants processes, notably the introduction of continuous *Australian Research Council (ARC) Linkage Projects* grant rounds and fast track decision-making (Box 2.4), are also expected to increase incentives for collaborative research and commercialisation, as they allow both researchers and industry partners to take a greater advantage of emerging innovation opportunities (Watt, 2015b; Australian Government, 2015a).

Inadequate support for indirect research costs (e.g. overheads, facilities and equipment) is seen by some universities as constraining resources (including staff time and funding) for collaboration and commercialisation of research (Go8, 2015; The University of Sydney, 2015). Currently, the indirect costs of research projects funded by the Australian competitive grants are met by the RBG (Box 2.1). However, some argue that the block grants fail to do this adequately (see for example, Williams, 2016). In addition, it has been argued that the lack of an integrated mechanism for funding the direct and indirect costs of research makes it difficult to obtain a consistent and full funding of research projects (AAMRI, 2006). The Watt Review concluded that, in spite of concerns, the present level of support for the indirect costs of research has not affected the quality of research to date, though it did call for monitoring to ensure that this will remain the case (Watt, 2015b).

Consideration could also be given to introducing incentives in the university funding system for R&D expenditure in fields with the greatest potential gains from collaborative activity, such as engineering and technology, and information technology (Williams, 2016). Australian institutions rank poorly internationally with regards to the R&D expenditure in these fields (Figure 2.14).

Figure 2.14. **University R&D expenditure on engineering and technology is low**

Share of higher education R&D expenditure by field of science, 2013 or latest

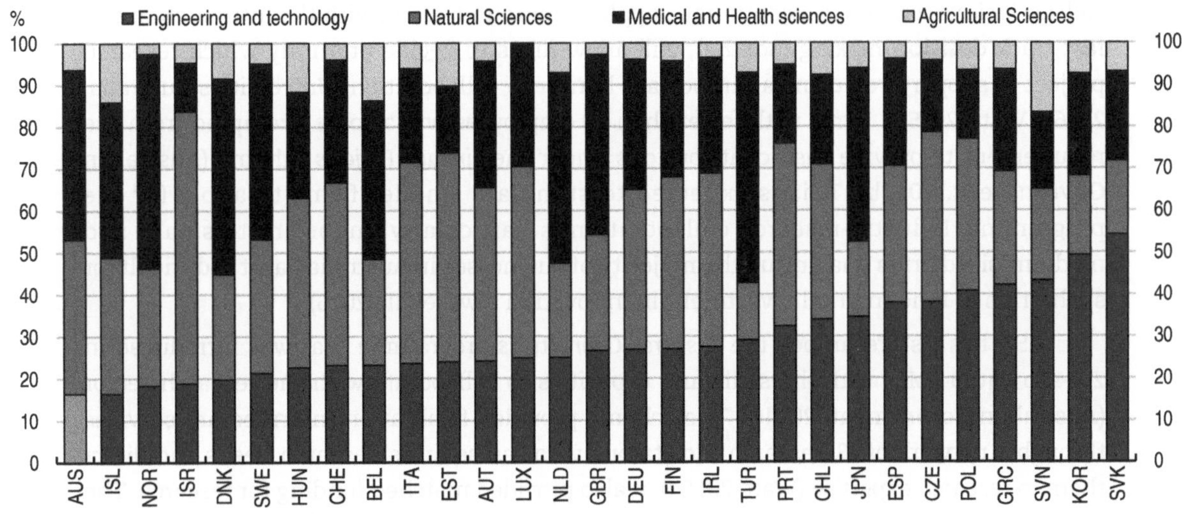

Source: OECD (2016), Research and Development Statistics (database).

StatLink ⟨⟨⟨⟨ http://dx.doi.org/10.1787/888933457207

The government should also proceed with the development of the new "impact assessment" model, taking into account the lessons from the pilot in 2017 (Box 2.4). As noted in Box 2.4, Australia has a national evaluation framework for the quality of the university research, but an impact and engagement framework that would allow an assessment of the economic and social benefits of such research is missing. The challenges of developing the new impact assessment model should not be underestimated. Transparent, well-designed, evidence-supported, monetary and non-monetary indicators are important in this regard (Jensen and Webster, 2016; Go8, 2015). These would help to monitor better how well (or otherwise) the universities are translating their research outcomes into wider impacts, which would increase accountability with regard to the value of publicly funded research and facilitate better-informed funding decisions (Penfield et al., 2014). Moreover, the new model is expected to provide universities impetus for increased engagement with industry and other end-users of research, enhancing knowledge transfer.

Encouraging business to become more active in collaborative research

Boosting collaboration also requires effective incentives to stimulate industry to seek research partnerships. The federal government supports a number of business-focused collaboration programmes. These include: the *Rural Research and Development Corporations* (Box 2.1); the *Cooperative Research Centres* (Box 2.1); and the *ARC Linkage* schemes. In addition, there are programmes (such as *Innovation Connections*, discussed below) that assist firms, mainly SMEs, to connect with research institutions. According to the information cited by the Watt Review, around 1 800 businesses were involved in government-funded collaboration programmes in 2013-14 (excluding those administrated by the Department of Agriculture), which corresponds to only 13% of the firms registered under the *R&D Tax Incentive* scheme (Watt, 2015b).

Recent initiatives under the *National Innovation and Science Agenda* (NISA) go in the right direction towards boosting business-led research partnerships. The move of the ARC *Linkage Projects* scheme to a continuous application round, along with the introduction of a fast-track decision-making (Box 2.4), will allow firms to decide promptly which research project to support, removing an important barrier to collaboration (Universities Australia, 2016a; Watt, 2015b). Firms with fewer than 20 employees will also be exempted from the requirement to provide cash contributions under the *Linkage Projects* scheme (Australian Government, 2016b). This is expected to stimulate smaller firms to apply for the programme. Industry-research collaboration is particularly important to small- and medium-sized firms (making up the majority of businesses in Australia), as it is difficult for such firms to fund internal investment in innovation (PwC et al., 2015).

NISA has also revamped the *Research Connections* programme that was introduced in 2014 to equip SMEs with the skills and capacities to collaborate with the research sector (Australian Government, 2014d). The scheme provided facilitation/intermediary services through a network of 13 Research Facilitators, who assess firms' research needs and direct them to research expertise (Watt, 2015b). It also provided matched funding for research. The new programme, *Innovation Connections* (launched in early 2016), expands the support. There will be eight new Innovation Facilitators and two new grant components. The latter extend the support for placements, notably of graduate or post-graduate researchers in businesses and of business researchers in a publicly funded research organisation (Australian Government, 2015a). *Innovation Connections* is part of the broader *Entrepreneurs' Programme* which provides practical support for businesses, researchers and entrepreneurs.

The *Innovation Connections* programme can assist more SMEs to "reach into" institutions that have the skills to address their research needs, particularly in regional Australia. Evidence suggests that such types of programmes can encourage partnerships between SMEs and research institutions which are likely to continue after the completion of the grant project (Watt, 2015b). A close monitoring of the revamped scheme is necessary in view of the relatively low take-up rates of the government-funded business-focused collaboration programmes. The evaluation results should be published for transparency. Simple and flexible governance and management arrangements are also important, helping to avoid unnecessary delays in the negotiation and formalisation of agreements for collaborative research (OECD, 2012). The success of collaboration-enhancing schemes further hinges upon the stability in the programmes offered, as frequent changes in the design and naming can reduce effectiveness.

An effective and efficient system of business-focused collaboration programmes also requires co-ordination among different levels of government. At present, broadly similar schemes to *Innovation Connections* (a national programme) are operated by some state governments, for instance *Technovouchers* in New South Wales and the *Innovation Vouchers Programme* in Western Australia (Watt, 2015b). This increases the risk of overlap and increased administrative costs. The new framework (discussed below) developed by the Department of Industry, Innovation and Science for the evaluation and measurement of programmes and policies (Australian Government, 2015b) is a welcome step towards an effective management and better co-ordination.

These initiatives need to be complemented by reforms in the *R&D Tax Incentive* scheme, providing financial support for business R&D, to better incentivise industry to collaborate with the research sector (see below).

2. BOOSTING R&D OUTCOMES

Ensuring a more effective management of IP by universities

Universities have introduced simplified IP licencing processes in recent years to promote collaborative research. Seven universities are currently members of *Easy Access IP* – an international network offering a free licence to a specific technology, using a simple, non-negotiable one-page agreement (Eggington et al., 2015; Watt, 2015a,b). *Easy Access IP* allows companies (or individuals) to evaluate and commercialise university research output quickly. Business must pay for the patenting costs and acknowledge the university as the source of the IP. If not commercialised within three years, the IP reverts back to the university. Irrespective, the universities can use the IP for research and teaching purposes (Watt, 2015b; PC, 2016). Also, all universities have signed up to use *Source IP*, a central platform aiming to provide information to business about public sector IP. Finally, the government has developed the *IP Toolkit* (launched in September 2015) to simplify and improve the management and use of IP in partnerships between businesses and researchers (Australian Government, 2015c). The Toolkit offers guidance about potential collaborators and contract negotiations and also provides the tools (including a model contract) necessary for streamlining the process of collaborative IP arrangements.

Furthermore, the funding arrangements for Australian competitive grants are to be amended in 2017, as was recommended by the Watt Review, requiring universities to list their patents generated by publicly funded research on *Source IP* and offer, and use, if requested by the collaborative partners, simplified contracting arrangements (in particular, the *IP Toolkit* model contract) (Watt, 2015b; Australian Government, 2016b). The government will also require all future applications and progress reports for the ARC *Linkage Projects* scheme – designed for collaborative research – to identify the actual and potential IP arising from the project and planned management arrangements.

These initiatives go in the right direction. Further development and wider use of simplified contracts, such as those incorporated in the *IP Toolkit* and *Easy Access IP*, is critical for knowledge exchange and collaboration on the exploitation of IP. For instance, an assessment of the *Easy Access IP* scheme in the United Kingdom for the period 2012-15 found that it has resulted in savings in staff time and legal costs (Eggington et al., 2015). The Watt Review's assessment of *Easy Access IP* also concluded that it usefully supports the commercialisation of university research and that the broader application of *Easy Access IP*, or similar arrangements, should be investigated (Watt, 2015b).

Open access publishing is also being strengthened. In 2013, Australia introduced limited open access policies, aiming to improve access to publications arising from research supported by public funding (through the *Australian Research Council* and the *National Health and Medical Research Council*, see Box 2.1) (Watt, 2015b). In line with the recommendation of the Watt Review, reporting arrangements for universities will consider the relative share of research output made available through publication or open source repositories. Some countries further include "use it or lose it" provisions for IP in research funding arrangements, which allow public funders to appropriate IP if its owner is not exploiting it, although the Productivity Commission did not find supporting evidence for the introduction of such provisions in universities (PC, 2016) (Box 2.5).

The steps to strengthen open access publishing are welcome. Several studies show that open access publishing improves the impact of scientific papers (OECD, 2015a), although challenges remain, including the risk of dissemination of lower-quality scientific results and the need to make it more sustainable through market mechanisms, as most

> **Box 2.5. The pros and cons of a "use it or lose it" scheme for publicly funded IP in universities**
>
> The 2015 *Review of Research Policy and Funding Arrangements* (Watt Review) recommended the authorities examine the feasibility of a "use it or lose it" scheme (Watt, 2015b). Such provisions would require a university to free up the IP arising from publicly funded projects if commercialisation does not begin within a specific time frame.
>
> In principle, a "use it or lose it" scheme could strengthen access to IP; however, there are design and enforcement issues. Choosing an appropriate time deadline is challenging as the "reasonable" time frame for commercialisation will vary widely across research projects. A "use it or lose it" scheme also increases complexity in reporting arrangements (Watt, 2015b). Moreover, the compulsory licence arrangements for patents in Australia, which also apply to publicly funded organisations, imply already de facto "use it or lose it" arrangement for patents owned by such organisations, weakening the rational for additional provisions (PC, 2016). On balance, the Productivity Commission found a lack of evidence for more interventionist approaches of IP arising from publicly funded research, advocating instead that existing measures such as *Easy Access IP* and *Source IP*, which are still at a preliminary stage, should be given time to work before additional measures are considered.

open-access journals rely on subsidies or funding from universities and government (OECD, 2015a). In its recent study on IP arrangements, the Productivity Commission recommends that the federal and state governments provide free access through an open access repository for all publicly funded publications, within 12 months of publication (PC, 2016). This would facilitate further knowledge exchange.

Australia's Technology Transfer Offices (TTOs) are specialised in the creation, management and enforcement of IP rights (PC, 2016). Some Australian TTOs have been successful, but there is scope for improvement. TTO's managerial capacities have been criticised, including a lack of "genuine" support for commercialisation efforts and limited skills in the management of IP and licensing and start-ups (Harman, 2010). More recently, Jensen and Webster (2016) have underscored the importance of legal teams specialised in unconventional outputs, such as databases, algorithms and apps that are neither patentable nor can be clearly protected by copyright. Overall, therefore there appears room for TTOs to become more effective.

Removing barriers to industry-relevant research training and mobility between sectors

Industry experience, especially for young researchers, is an important channel for linking universities and businesses (PwC et al., 2015). According to a recent review by the Australian Council of Learned Academies (ACOLA), several factors dissuade the creation of industry placements for higher degree research students, including inflexibilities in rules governing the scholarship schemes for post-graduate students and high financial and administrative costs of placements for business (McGagh, et al., 2016).

Moreover, Australia lacks a co-ordinated approach to industry placements for higher degree research students, and so the proposal by the ACOLA review for a nationally consistent approach is welcome. This would reduce complexity and red-tape burden on universities and industry partners and allow researchers to obtain better information about appropriate placement opportunities. It would also increase accountability (McGagh, et al., 2016). Besides boosting collaboration, industry-relevant research experience could improve employment opportunities beyond academia. Furthermore, innovation-relevant skills and university-business linkages can be strengthened through encouraging students to take "entrepreneurship" courses as part of their degrees. In the Netherlands, for example, nearly all Universities and Universities of Applied Sciences are offering entrepreneurship units in degree courses (Chapter 1).

Plans to revise, through engagement with universities, the appointment and promotion arrangements for academics, so that time spent in business is given greater recognition, go in the right direction (Australian Government, 2016b). This would lessen the link between promotion opportunities and publication outcomes, promoting mobility between the research and industry sectors. It is important that the new appointment and promotion policies are carefully designed, entailing "engagement" criteria that attach high weights to industry experience with large potential for facilitating knowledge flow.

More information on research outcomes and expertise would also facilitate mobility between business and research sectors. Ongoing development of an online access point to connect businesses with commercially-relevant research and potential research partners is welcome (Watt, 2015b). Last, but not least, policy changes need to be accompanied by a shift in academic culture, which conventionally recognises only publications and teaching as "worthy" activities for career advancements (Jensen and Webster, 2016). The reform underway in funding arrangements for university research (Box 2.4) aims to prompt such change. At the same time, the businesses sector also needs to be open in offering work experience to researchers (PwC et al., 2015).

The need for an integrated approach across research, innovation and education (the so-called "knowledge triangle") is well recognised by the OECD countries, given the systemic nature of innovation and the role – and relationship – of the different players in the innovation system. Research hubs, such as the Waterloo knowledge triangle in Canada (see OECD, 2016 for further discussion), can provide useful examples for Australia.

Achieving greater commercial impact from Australia's public-sector research

The Commonwealth Scientific and Industrial Research Organisation (CSIRO) (Box 2.6) is the largest public-sector (non-defence) research agency in Australia. It undertakes multidisciplinary in-house research and collaboration with other research partners, including universities and industries, as well as international partners (PC, 2007). Overall, CSIRO performs well, meeting expectations and targets in performance indicators for its main programmes. Various evaluations have concluded that, overall, CSIRO brings net benefit (see for instance, ACIL Tasman, 2010 and ACIL Allen, 2014). Moreover, programmes administrated by CSIRO, such as the *SME Engagement Centre*, connecting business to expertise and government programmes, seem to be working well. Existing data suggest that, since 2008, the programme has helped more than 100 SMEs to grow and become more competitive (Watt, 2015b).

There is scope, however, for further improving CSIRO's effectiveness in terms of commercialisation of its research and knowledge transfer, while ensuring that this does not come at the cost of excellence in research or societal impacts. The agency ranks among the world's top 25 government research organisations on the basis of the Reuter's ranking of innovative capacity and achievement, and it also fares well in terms of "academic

> ## Box 2.6. **CSIRO: main features**
>
> The Commonwealth Scientific and Industrial Research Organisation (CSIRO) is an independent statutory body and the leading public sector research agency in Australia. It is a "mission directed" organisation with a primary remit to conduct research for the public good and assist Australian industry (OECD, 2011). CSIRO's remit also notably includes a responsibility to encourage the application or utilisation of the results of its research. Secondary functions include international scientific liaison, training of research workers, publication of research results, technology transfer of other research, provision of scientific services and dissemination of information about science and technology. CSIRO undertakes research across many areas, employing around 5000 employees (full-time equivalent), located in over 50 locations (CSIRO, 2015a, 2016). The wide variety of research projects and large scale of the agency provides considerable scope for multidisciplinary research to be carried in-house, reinforced through collaborative research (PC, 2007).
>
> In 2015-16 CSIRO received over 40% of the federal funding to public-sector research agencies (PSRAs) and close to 8% of the government's total support for science and innovation (Australian Government, 2016c). Around 62% of the agency's operating revenues in that year came through the federal budget, with the rest from external sources, including consulting and royalty and license revenues (CSIRO, 2016). CSIRO allocates its public funding using multiple criteria and with guidance from the *National Science and Research Priorities*. As of 2013, CSIRO has a statutory requirement to develop a *Corporate Plan* (a rolling 4-year plan) each year and submit an annual *Portfolio Budget Statement* (CSIRO, 2015b). Performance is assessed in *CSIRO's Annual Report*. Performance criteria (as from 2016-17 and beyond) include evidence of economic, social and environmental impacts, customer and user satisfaction, level of external revenue and improvement of innovation capacity. The performance of the *CSIRO Innovation Fund* (see below) is also assessed with regard to investments in science-based technology in industry sectors that have been identified as growth sectors for the Australian economy (Australian Government, 2016d).

impact" (Figure 2.3, Panel B). However, it lags behind comparable institutes in other countries in terms of "commercial impact", as proxied by the citation of its academic papers in patent filings (Figure 2.9, Panel D). This finding is supported by indicators showing that CSIRO's innovation outcomes fall behind its research excellence (Figure 2.15).

CSIRO has implemented in recent years a framework to plan, monitor and evaluate the impact of its research (CSIRO, 2014). This system tracks the translation of research into benefits ("pathways to impact") and is based on the "Triple Bottom Line" (TBL) approach. TBL is an internationally recognised impact assessment framework with three dimensions: environmental, social, and economic. CSIRO uses both cost-benefit analysis (usually for economic impacts), in addition to more qualitative methods (CSIRO, 2015c). Evaluations are based on internal or external assessments, or a mix of the two types. The framework includes both planning (ex-ante) and evaluation (retrospective).

The move to a more comprehensive and consistent impact evaluation approach is welcome. The new framework can help CSIRO better plan and measure the impact of its research. In addition, the new approach will enable improved aggregation and comparison of outcomes/impact across the organisation. However, so far, the impact evaluation has been retrospective. Progress needs to be made towards future impact planning as well. This is particularly important in view of the larger focus given, compared to the past, on the

Figure 2.15. **The commercial impact of public-sector research could be strengthened**

Ranking of CSIRO among world research institutions[1]

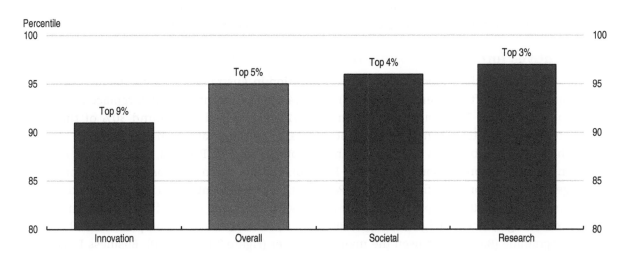

1. The "innovation" measure consists of innovative knowledge (scientific publication output from an institution cited in patents) and technological impact (percentage of the scientific publication output cited in patents). The "societal" measure consists of web size and domain's inbound links. The "research" measure consists of output, collaboration, research excellence, leadership and talent pool.

Source: Scimago Lab (2016), Scimago Institutions Rankings.

StatLink ⬛⬛⬛ http://dx.doi.org/10.1787/888933457217

commercial outcomes of research under CSIRO's new long-term strategy (CSIRO, 2015d; The Senate, 2015). It is welcome that CSIRO is releasing a new training programme focusing on impact pathways. It is important that planning and evaluation processes assess the wider impact of commercialisation, including the effect on research excellence and societal outcomes.

A new fund (the *CSIRO Innovation Fund*), announced as part of NISA, was launched at end-2016 by the government to support early stage commercialisation of research from CSIRO, other research institutions and universities (Australian Government, 2015a). The fund has two components: *i)* an early stage innovation fund of AUD 200 million to support co-investment in new spin-off and start-up companies created by research institutions; and, *ii)* a AUD 20 million strengthening of CSIRO's "accelerator programme" which assists preparation for commercial adoption. The early stage innovation fund will be co-funded by the government (AUD 70 million over 10 years), CSIRO and the private sector.

The establishment of the *CSIRO Innovation Fund* is a positive step given the important role of capital at the early stages of the commercialisation process, especially for start-ups. It will also foster greater research-industry collaboration. Investments by the *CSIRO Innovation Fund* need to carefully target projects with large commercialisation and productivity-enhancing potential. The new performance criteria for CSIRO (Box 2.6) are a welcome step forward. As the fund is still at its initial phase, a close follow up of outcomes would be advisable.

Effectiveness and efficiency of public-sector research should be improved further by the ongoing implementation of the *Public Governance, Performance and Accountability Act 2013* (PGPA Act) under which public-sector research entities are required to measure and assess their performance. The Act introduces obligations for annual performance statements (to be tabled in Parliament) and a *Corporate Plan*, as is currently the practice by CSIRO (Box 2.6).

A common approach to assessing the outcomes and impacts of research of PSRAs will bring more accurate measurement of the benefits of public funding for research (CSIRO 2015c), also helping to improve Australia's commercialisation and innovation outcomes. Ensuring a swift transition by PSRAs to the new arrangements is important.

Tax incentives form the core of Australia's financial support for business R&D

Most financial support for business innovation in Australia comes via the *R&D Tax Incentive* (hereafter, Incentive) (Box 2.7). In 2014-15, the Incentive, which replaced the long-lived *R&D Tax Concession* scheme in 2011, accounted for around 30% of the government's total expenditure in science, research and innovation, and for over 90% of the support for business research and innovation (Figure 2.16, Panel A), which is high in international comparison (Figure 2.16, Panel B). The tax incentives for SMEs are more generous than for larger firms (Box 2.7). Participation in the Incentive has increased rapidly since its introduction, particularly for SMEs, with the fiscal costs of the programme exceeding forecasts (Figure 2.17, Panels A to C). The refundable component of the programme (Box 2.7) has been the main cost driver (Figure 2.17, Panel D). Business R&D intensity data have so far not echoed this development (Figure 2.17, Panel B). This possibly reflects other influences, especially the end of the mining boom (Box 2.2). Regardless, this trend needs to be closely monitored, and included in assessments of the programme's effectiveness in encouraging additional business R&D.

Box 2.7. **R&D Tax Incentive: main features**

The *R&D Tax Incentive* (Incentive), introduced in 2011, provides tax offsets to incorporated companies for R&D activity, including foreign companies that are tax resident in Australia (Ferris et al., 2016). Trusts are generally not eligible to claim the Incentive.

The programme is jointly administered by AusIndustry (on behalf of Innovation and Science Australia) and the Australian Taxation Office (ATO). In broad terms, AusIndustry manages the registration of companies accessing the Incentive and determines the eligibility of R&D activities, while ATO determines the eligibility of companies applying for the scheme and the eligibility of their claimed R&D expenditure (Australian Government, 2015d; Ferris et al., 2016). The Incentive is a self-assessment programme, the ATO and AusIndustry undertake compliance activities as part of their administration of the Incentive.

The Incentive has two components:

- a 43.5 % refundable tax credit (offset) (45% prior to July 2016) for eligible companies with an aggregated turnover of less than AUD 20 million per annum. The refundable element of the scheme means that, where a company's tax liability is smaller than the value of the R&D tax offset, they receive an immediate refund, rather than carrying forward the offsets;

- a non-refundable 38.5% tax credit (offset) (40% prior to July 2016) for eligible companies with an aggregated turnover of AUD 20 million or more per annum.

An annual AUD 100 million R&D expenditure threshold was introduced 2015. Firms with eligible R&D above the threshold receive, from July 2014, a tax credit at the prevailing company tax rate (30%) rather than the Incentive rate (Australian Government, 2016e).

Figure 2.16. **Government support for business R&D: trends and international comparisons**

A. Tax support for business R&D

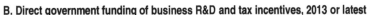
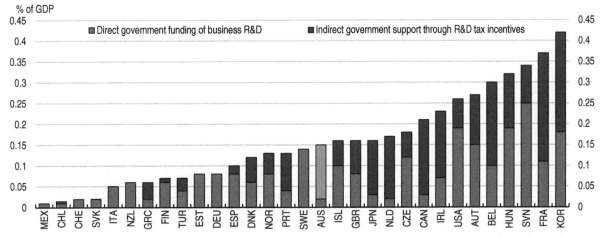

B. Direct government funding of business R&D and tax incentives, 2013 or latest

Source: Australian Department of Industry, Innovation and Science (2016), Science, Research and Innovation Budget Tables; OECD (2015), OECD Science, Technology and Industry Scoreboard 2015, Chapter 4.

StatLink ⟨≡⟩ http://dx.doi.org/10.1787/888933457224

There are challenges in making the R&D Tax Incentive more effective

A key measure of effectiveness of public support to R&D is "additionality": the extent to which the support prompts R&D over-and-above the amount which would be undertaken without it. Evidence suggests that only around 10-20% of the total R&D registered under the Incentive is additional, a similar result to that found in other countries (Australian Government, 2016e). An assessment of the Incentive (Ferris et al., 2016), as part of a government-initiated review, concluded that the programme "falls short of its stated objectives of additionality and spillovers".

Strengthening additionality may be difficult. By design, volume-based (i.e. applying to all qualified R&D expenditure) tax instruments, such as the Incentive, not only subsidise the additional R&D but also support the activities which would have been conducted in the absence of tax incentives (Appelt et al., 2016; Ferris et al., 2016). This puts limits on the additionality that can be achieved. Furthermore, measures that endeavour to raise additionality (such as, more sophisticated eligibility criteria) can increase complexity, and

Figure 2.17. **Cost developments of the of R&D Tax Incentive**

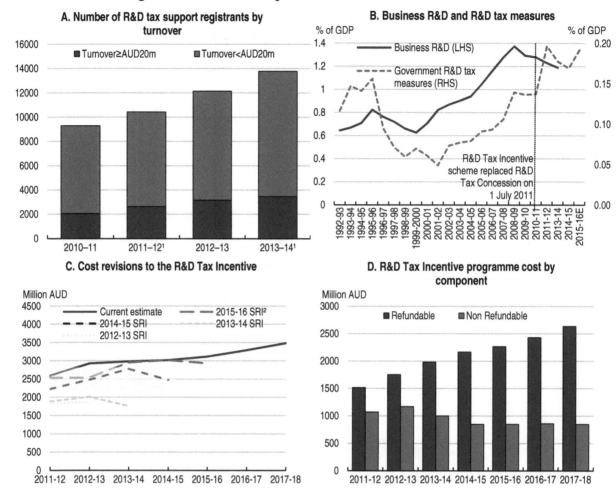

1. 2011-12 was a transitional year in which some firms accessed the R&D Tax Concession while others accessed the R&D Tax Incentive and 2013-14 data are not complete.
2. Australian Government's Science, Research and Innovation (SRI) budget.
Source: Ferris et al. (2016), Review of the R&D Tax Incentive; Department of Industry, Innovation and Science (2015), Innovation Australia: Annual Report 2014-15; ABS (2015), 8104.0 – Research and Experimental Development, Businesses, Australia, 2013-14.

StatLink ⟨⟩ http://dx.doi.org/10.1787/888933457237

consequently, compliance and administrative costs. Among the reform options, one possibility would be to grant a part of the refundable R&D incentive (see Box 2.7) under more stringent criteria for additionality (see for example, KPMG, 2016). While of merit, designing (and implementing) the additional criteria may be challenging and may add to the high administrative burden.

Another reform option to sharpen focus on additional R&D activity is to introduce an intensity threshold. Ferris et al. (2016), for instance, recommend only applying the tax credit to R&D spending that exceeds 1-2% of total business expenses for the recipients of the non-refundable component (larger companies) of the Incentive. If well implemented, such a reform could make the Incentive more targeted, increasing its effectiveness. Evaluation and, if needed, adjustment will be important as experience is gained. Complementing this recommendation, Ferris et al. suggest doubling the existing expenditure threshold (from AUD 100 million to AUD 200 million) in order for large R&D-intensive firms to retain an incentive to undertake additional R&D.

Making the *R&D Tax Incentive* a more effective instrument for collaborative research between businesses and publicly funded research institutions is also important, given that such research is more likely to generate spillovers (Appelt et al., 2016). Indeed, recent firm-level evidence suggests that Australian firms that innovate and source their ideas from research organisations are 34% more productive than those that do not (ACOLA, 2014). Currently, the Incentive does not focus on encouraging collaboration; in 2013-14 only 9.5% of projects under the programme were involved in collaboration with another organisation (Australian Government, 2016e). The government could consider introducing an R&D tax-credit premium for business expenditure on collaborative research with publicly funded research organisations, or add criteria relating to collaboration in the eligibility criteria for the current programme. Various analyses (see for example, PwC et al., 2015; ATN, 2016; Ferris et al., 2016; Universities Australia, 2016b), favour an R&D tax-credit premium option for Australia. Ferris et al. specifically recommend an additional premium rate of tax credit of up to 20% above the current non-refundable tax credit rate where R&D expenditure involves collaboration with publicly funded research organisations. Several other OECD countries use R&D tax incentives to promote collaboration (Appelt et al., 2016). For example, in Japan, the tax credit rate is increased to 30% for joint R&D activity with a university or public research institutions (the standard credit is 12% for SMEs and 8-10% for large firms) (OECD, 2015c). In Canada, eligible corporations in Ontario can claim a 20% (capped) refundable tax credit for research performed under contract with eligible research institutes (Ontario Ministry of Finance, 2014).

An R&D tax-credit premium could also increase mobility between the industry and research sectors, if eligibility for the premium included exchange of staff between the industry and research partners (ATN, 2016; Universities Australia, 2016b), and/or R&D tax incentives were strengthened for firms employing PhD graduates for a specific period after graduation (PwC et al., 2015; Ferris et al., 2016). Ferris et al. recommend, for instance, that the collaboration premium of up to 20% for the non-refundable tax credit (see above) also applies to the cost of employing recent PhD, or equivalent, graduates in science, technology, engineering or maths (STEM) in their first three years of employment. Mechanisms aiming to increase employment of researchers in industry operate elsewhere. For instance, in France wage expenditures of researchers with a PhD or equivalent degree are considered twice for R&D credit purposes during the first 24 months following their first recruitment (OECD, 2015c). Other mechanisms for R&D business support, such as grants, could also be used to encourage collaboration, complementing the *R&D Tax Incentive* (Deloitte, 2016). The exchange of staff, for instance, can also be directly supported.

In view of the importance of the *R&D Tax Incentive* in Australia's innovation policy, and the significant budgetary costs involved, comprehensive analyses are required for assessing additionality. This could include, without underestimating the measurement difficulties, an evaluation not only of "input" but also "output" additionality (the outputs from R&D activities which would not have been achieved without public support), accompanied by estimates of wider economic and social benefits (Appelt et al., 2016). Publishing the results of such analyses would increase transparency regarding the performance of the *R&D Tax Incentive*, making it easier to communicate any policy changes. Evaluations should also look at the possible trade-off between increasing additionality and complexity. The OECD has launched a project to evaluate R&D tax credit systems across countries using micro-data (Appelt et al., 2016).

Ensuring integrity and containing cost

Efficiency and effectiveness of the R&D tax break system further hinges upon ensuring high standards of integrity in the use of funds. Both AusIndustry and ATO undertake compliance activities as part of their administration of the Incentive (Box 2.7). AusIndustry's risk review activities focus on the risk of non-compliance of registered R&D activities at the pre-registration or post-registration stages. In the case of ATO, compliance activities are concentrated primarily on expenditure and the behaviour of specialist tax advisers (Ferris et al., 2016). The findings of AusIndustry's and the ATO's compliance activities suggest that most participants in the Incentive programme are acting in accordance with the programme's rules. Specific delivery risks have been identified, however. Incorrectly identifying activities as research and development and/or incorrectly attributing expenditure against activities is one of the major risks to the integrity of the programme. This issue needs to be monitored closely, introducing, if necessary, tighter compliance measures that are well-targeted. Developing comprehensive data sets that help gauge the extent of the abuse is also important.

The introduction of the *R&D Tax Incentive* in 2011 brought new definitions of core and supporting R&D activity, which are welcome as they aim at increasing clarity (Australian Government, 2016e). The R&D eligibility conditions reflect the principles in the *OECD Frascati Manual* (OECD, 2015d), used by several countries as a basis for identifying R&D activity and expenditure. The eligibility conditions essentially require the development of new knowledge, a purpose and systematic approach to develop such knowledge, and an element of technical risk regarding the success of the approach (Ferris et al., 2016). The Incentive's eligibility criteria are principle-based, providing flexibility for changing R&D activities over time. However, such an approach can be open to misinterpretation and possible "boundary pushing" of eligibility (Australian Government, 2016e). The 2012 *Survey* (OECD, 2012) highlighted the need for clear and consistent interpretation by those processing applications of the eligibility criteria and frequent evaluation of outcomes. The recent assessment of the Incentive by Ferris et al. specifically recommends the development of new guidance (including plain-language summaries and case studies) to increase clarity about the scope of eligible activities and expenses.

The upward risks to the costs of the Incentive could be further managed by strengthening provisions for the existing expenditure cap, applying it to "connected entities", and/or by introducing additional caps (BDO, 2016). For instance, a cap on the refundable component of the Incentive (applicable to smaller firms) could be considered, with any amounts above the cap to be retained by the firm as a carried-forward non-refundable tax credit (see, BDO, 2016 and Ferris et al., 2016). In placing a cap on refundability it is important to assess carefully its potential trade-off with additionality, especially as there is some evidence that SMEs are more responsive than large firms to fiscal incentives (Australian Government, 2016e).

Enhancing administrative efficiency

There is also scope for improving the administrative efficiency of the Incentive programme. Compliance costs for the participating firms are relatively high as a percentage of the financial support provided, standing, on average, at 23% for small firms and 8% for large companies (Ferris et al., 2016). Such costs include time and resources to complete the application process and to keep records for the justification of activities and respond to audits. The fees paid by participating firms to consultants (specialist advisers), according to available information, account for almost half of the total compliance costs. This may reflect issues with the clarity or complexity of the Incentive, prompting the need for specialist advisers to help optimise companies' returns from the Incentive. In a review of the programme in 2015, stakeholders stressed the scope for reducing compliance costs by streamlining the application process (Australian Government, 2016e). Currently, companies first register the R&D activities they have self-assessed and then make the claim for tax return. As a reform option, the government could consider adopting a single application process for accessing the *R&D Tax Incentive*, as was also suggested by Ferris et al. Further benefits could be derived by developing a combined database by the two agencies (see Box 2.7) administrating the programme (Ferris et al., 2016).

The process for registering an R&D activity raises additional issues. Under present arrangements, the tax support is claimed *ex post*, i.e. after the R&D spending has taken place. Specifically, a firm has 10 months after the end of an income year to register R&D activities (Australian Government, 2016e). Some argue that this encourages claims for "business-as-usual" costs that do not represent the type of R&D targeted by the Incentive. A pre-registration process for R&D activity could lessen this problem, as it would require firms to identify specific projects that they would later make a claim for (ATSE, 2016); but such process could also add to the administrative burden on firms, and could be complex to be administrated if firms had to change their planning (Deloitte, 2016).

The review of the *R&D Tax Incentive* provided an opportunity to consider reforms that would maximise the returns of public investment in business R&D, including through a better co-ordination of the Incentive with other initiatives in the innovation agenda. However, reform also needs to take account of the importance of stability, so that businesses can plan R&D spending without having to accommodate regulatory risk. The *OECD Innovation Imperative* (OECD, 2015a) cites evidence suggesting that frequent R&D policy changes undermine the effectiveness of R&D tax credits (Westmore, 2013). The review of the Incentive sensibly proposes fine-tuning the system rather than wholesale change. At the same time, a systematic evaluation of the programme is essential to assess whether or not it remains relevant and to identify corrective measures.

Is there a case of rebalancing the mix of support?

A shift in the balance between indirect (tax incentives) and direct support (grants) for business R&D could also be considered. R&D tax incentives do not have the "picking winners" problem associated with direct grants and require fewer administrative resources to operate compared to grants (OECD, 2015e). However, as discussed above, the evidence suggests that tax incentives are not hugely efficient in terms of additionality, although this depends on design (Appelt et al., 2016). Grants or other forms of direct support can be more efficient, as these can be focussed on areas that might have particularly high additionality. Recent OECD analysis also suggests direct support measures may be more effective in inducing R&D than previously considered, especially in the case of young firms where lack of upfront funds for an innovative project is often a barrier. Furthermore, whereas R&D tax incentives are also more likely to stimulate short-term applied research and boost incremental innovation, direct subsidies are more targeted towards long-term research and radical innovations. However, the fund allocation process must be based on rigorous and transparent criteria, while the selection process should ensure efficiency and avoid rent-seeking activities and adverse selection problems (OECD, 2015a).

Enhancing coherence and co-ordination in the science, research and innovation system

A complex system with many players

Several government departments at the federal level and numerous councils, committees and boards are involved in the science, research and innovation system (Green, 2015). State governments are also involved in policy development and programme design. Federal government investment in research and innovation is spread across 15 portfolios, with their own research and innovation programmes and multiple agencies delivering such programmes (Cutler, 2008). Major research agencies, namely the *Australian Research Council* (ARC) and the *National Health and Medical Research Council* (NHMRC), do not directly conduct research but they influence the national research programme through the funding they provide to universities and medical research institutes.

A more co-ordinated approach would be welcome. A recent inquiry stressed the need for a more integrated, "whole-of-government", approach to science, research and innovation (The Senate, 2015). The consultation report highlights fragmentation in decision-making and resource allocation between many government departments and research funding agencies, as well as frequent changes in the functions and structure of departments and a lack of regular, independent evaluations. It calls for the establishment of strategic goals in key areas, eliminating duplication and overlap and ensuring continuity and outcome-orientation in policies and programmes across the whole of government.

Reforms underway could go further

A new independent board, *Innovation and Science Australia* (ISA), was established in 2016 that has roles: *i)* to provide strategic whole-of-government advice on the government's investment in science, research and innovation; and, *ii)* to oversee the operational delivery of a number of programs (Box 2.8; Australian Government, 2015a). Through the provision of coordinated data and advice, this new board will assist government to make better informed decisions about investment in science, research and innovation, and help plan such investment in light of national priorities (Australian Government, 2015a). ISA will

---

Box 2.8. **Innovation and Science Australia**

A new statutory independent board, *Innovation and Science Australia* (ISA), was announced in December 2015, as part of the NISA, with responsibility for "strategic whole-of-government advice on all science, research and innovation matters" (Australian Government, 2015a). The relevant legislation for its establishment became effective in July 2016. The aim is for ISA to have a broader role than its predecessor, *Innovation Australia*. Notably, it will work across government and interact directly with stakeholders; audit and review regularly the innovation system to assess its performance and make recommendations to align government strategic priorities; and, develop a 15-year national plan for investment in science, research and innovation (Parliament of Australia, 2016). ISA will also continue to perform the work of its predecessor, including the administration, monitoring, oversight and operation of programmes such as the *R&D Tax Incentive* and the *Cooperative Research Centres* (CRC) programme. It will complement the *Commonwealth Science Council*, established in 2014 to advise the government on all aspects of science and technology in Australia.

---

conduct comprehensive audits and regular reviews of the innovation system, which can help identify possible gaps in and/or misalignment of strategic objectives. The 15-year plan for the government's investment in science, research and innovation that ISA is required to develop, will usefully help prioritise major research projects and reform initiatives.

Although is too early to assess the effectiveness of ISA, this reform holds promise in paving the way for a whole-of-government approach to science, research and innovation. ISA also has the potential for promoting collaboration, given that the new body will be working directly with the industry and community sectors. Such an engagement could in turn increase stakeholders' support for the government's innovation policies, and hence their successful implementation (OECD, 2015a). ISA's progress on these fronts needs to be closely monitored and evaluated. It is important to ensure that greater coordination does not come at the expense of the diversity of innovation activities, constraining the responsiveness of the science, research and innovation system to evolving needs (Cutler, 2008).

Steps towards a more coordinated and coherent system could further include abolishing or consolidating certain research programmes. The *National Commission of Audit* refers, for example, to the numerous (around 150) research funding programmes and agreements, many of which, in its view, are not well targeted or appear to have negligible positive spillovers (NCOA, 2014). Such programmes are spread across the various government agencies and departments. The Commission also saw scope for reducing administrative costs, proposing, for instance, a better aligning of ARC and NHMRC grant processes (but keeping the medical research funding pool separate).

Strengthening the monitoring and evaluation of innovation programmes

As mentioned in various places throughout this chapter, high quality evaluation and performance measurement is a precondition for effective innovation policy, as they are the basis for changes if outcomes are not in line with intentions. The difficulties in developing effective measures and key performance indicators should not be underestimated, especially when the outcomes of the publicly funded research appear only in the longer term. Good practice principles underscore that evaluations should be based on independent and transparent assessment; their findings are made public; and that they are accompanied by effective mechanisms for policy learning to ensure that the findings of evaluation are guiding future decision making (OECD, 2015a). The system should incorporate both *ex-post* and *ex-ante* evaluations (Appelt et al., 2016; OECD, 2014).

Recent steps towards improving evaluation performance, including the development of the new impact assessment for university research and the transitioning of public-sector research agencies and other Commonwealth entities to a common approach to assessing the outcomes and impact of research under the *Public Governance, Performance and Accountability Act 2013* (discussed above) are welcome. Notably, the *Evaluation Strategy 2015-19* of the Department of Industry, Innovation and Science, provides a framework to guide evaluation and performance measurement of its programmes and policies (Australian Government, 2015b). The strategy incorporates evaluation across a programme's lifecycle and envisages both prospective and retrospective evaluations. A core goal of the framework is to improve the data available to assess programmes' outcomes and impacts, an essential element for ensuring policy effectiveness.

Recommendations on boosting R&D outcomes

Strengthening the links between research and business sectors

- Put a greater weight, as envisaged, on collaboration in university funding, including increasing the role of income derived from research partnerships in determining research grants. Implement university funding reforms that introduce simplified arrangements for block funding.

- Develop a more coordinated approach to industry placements for higher degree research students.

- Encourage a greater weight for industry experience in the university appointment and promotion system.

- Increase the take-up rate of programmes that encourage business to collaborate by implementing simple and flexible governance arrangements and providing greater stability in the range of programmes.

- Improve the management of Intellectual Property (IP) created by university research, particularly by further developing simplified IP contracts and continuing to promote open access publishing.

Achieving greater commercial impact from public-sector research

- Implement a common approach across public-sector research agencies for assessing research outcomes and impacts.

- Ensure that investments by the *CSIRO Innovation Fund* target projects with large commercialisation and productivity-enhancing potential.

Enhancing the effectiveness and efficiency of the R&D Tax Incentive

- Make the Incentive more effective by adjusting its parameters, for example by:
  - ❖ Combining an eligibility threshold with an increase in the expenditure cap for recipients of non-refundable component of the Incentive (larger companies), as suggested in the recent review.
  - ❖ Granting a part of the refundable Incentive under more stringent criteria for additionality.
  - ❖ Consider introducing an R&D tax premium for business expenditure on collaborative research with publicly funded research institutions.

- To better manage the fiscal cost of the Incentive, consider placing a cap on the refundable component, with any amounts above the cap to be carried forward.

- Adopt a single application process for accessing the Incentive to lower compliance costs.

Reducing complexity in the governance of the science, research and innovation system

- Develop a more integrated, "whole-of-government", approach to science, research and innovation and consolidate innovation support programmes.

- Evaluate at an early stage the progress achieved towards greater co-ordination under the new innovation body, *Innovation and Science Australia*.

Improving evaluation performance and monitoring

- Strengthen the monitoring and evaluation of innovation programmes, in particular through the development of more comprehensive databases that provide input to the monitoring processes.

Bibliography

AAMRI (Association of Australian Medical Research Institutes) (2006), "Medical Research Institute Perspective on Public Support for Science and Innovation", Submission to the Productivity Commission's *Research Study on Public Support for Science and Innovation in Australia*, July.

ACIL Allen Consulting (2014), "CSIRO's Impact and Value – An Independent Assessment", December.

ACIL Tasman (2010), "Assessment of CSIRO Impact & Value", Report prepared as input to CSIRO's Lapsing Program Review, July.

ACIP (Advisory Council of Intellectual Property) (2012), *Collaborations Between the Public and Private Sectors: The Role of Intellectual Property*, Final Report, September.

ACOLA (Australian Council of Learned Academies) (2014), *Securing Australia's Future – The Role of Science, Research and Technology in Lifting Australian Productivity*, Final Report, June.

Allen Consulting Group (2012), "The Economic, Social and Environmental Impacts of the Cooperative Research Centres Program".

Ang, B. (2004), "Decomposition Analysis for Policymaking in Energy: Which is the Preferred Method?", *Energy Policy* 32, pp. 1131-39.

Appelt S., et al. (2016), "R&D Tax Incentives: Evidence on Design, Incidence and Impacts", *OECD Science, Technology and Industry Policy Papers*, No. 31.

ARC (Australian Research Council) (2016), "Excellence in Research for Australia", Australian Government, *www.arc.gov.au/excellence-research-australia*.

ATN (Australian Technology Network) (2016), "R&D Taxation Review", February, Canberra.

ATSE (Australia Academy of Technology and Engineering) (2016), "Submission to R&D Tax Incentive Review", February.

Australian Government (2011), *Focusing Australia's Publicly Funded Research Review – Maximising the Innovation Dividend: Review Key Findings and Future Directions*, October.

Australian Government (2014a), "Boosting the Commercial Returns from Research", October.

Australian Government (2014b), "Initiatives to Enhance the Professional Development of Research Students", June.

Australian Government (2014c), *Australian Innovation System Report 2014*, Commonwealth of Australia.

Australian Government (2014d), "Research Connections Fast-Tracks Business-Research Collaboration", September.

Australian Government (2015a), *National Innovation & Research Agenda*, Commonwealth of Australia.

Australian Government (2015b), *Evaluation Strategy 2015-19*, Commonwealth of Australia.

Australian Government (2015c), "Australian IP Toolkit for Collaboration", October.

Australian Government (2015d), "The R&D Tax Incentive: Overview", January.

Australian Government (2016a), "Cooperative Research Centres (CRC) Programme CRCs Over Time", Canberra.

Australian Government (2016b), "Delivering a High-Performing Research Sector in Australia: Watt Review Response", May.

Australian Government (2016c), *Science, Research and Innovation Budget Tables 2016-17*.

Australian Government (2016d), *Budget 2016-17: Industry, Innovation and Science Portfolio*, Commonwealth of Australia.

Australian Government (2016e), "R&D Tax Incentive Review Issues Paper", February.

Australian Universities (2014), "University Research: Policy Considerations to Drive Australia's Competitiveness", November.

BDO (2016), "R&D Tax Incentive Review – Issues Paper Response", February.

CO2CRC (2015), *Annual Report July-December 2014*, Melbourne.

CSIRO (Commonwealth Scientific and Industrial Research Organisation) (2014), *How CSIRO Ensures it Delivers Impact*, Canberra.

CSIRO (2015a), *Annual Report 2014-15 – Australia's Innovation Catalyst*, Canberra.

CSIRO (2015b), *Corporate Plan 2015-16 – Australia's Innovation Catalyst*, Canberra.

CSIRO (2015c), *Impact Evaluation Guide*, November, Canberra.

CSIRO (2015d), *Australia's Innovation Catalyst: CSIRO Strategy 2020*, July Canberra.

CSIRO (2016), *Annual Report 2015-16 – Australia's Innovation Catalyst*, Canberra.

Cutler, T. (2008), *Venturous Australia: Building Strength in Innovation*, Melbourne.

Deloitte (2016), "Submission re R&D Review and Issues Paper", February.

Eggington, E. et al. (2015), "Easy Access IP: A Preliminary Assessment of the Initiative", National Centre for Universities and Business, March.

Ferris B., Finkel A. and J. Fraser (2016), *Review of the R&D Tax Incentive*, April.

Go8 (Group of Eight) (2015), "Group of Eight Submission to the Review of Research Policy and Funding Arrangements for Higher Education", September.

Green, R. (2015), "Senate Inquiry into Australia's Innovation System – Issues Paper".

Harman, G. (2010),"Australian University Research Commercialisation: Perceptions of Technology Transfer Specialists and Science and technology Academics ", *Journal of Higher Education Policy and Management* Vol. 32, No. 1, February, 69–83.

Jensen, P. and E. Webster (2016), "Funding Research in Universities: The Watt Report 2015", *The Australian Economic Review*, Vol. 49, No. 2, pp. 184-91.

KPMG (2016), "R&D Tax Incentive Review: KPMG Response to Issues Paper", March.

McGagh, J. et al (2016), *Review of Australia's Research Training System*, Report for the Australian Council of Learned Academies (ACOLA).

NCOA (National Commission of Audit) (2014), *Towards Responsible Government: The Report of the National Commission of Audit*, Commonwealth of Australia, Canberra, February.

OECD (2011), *Public Research Institutions: Mapping Sector Trends*, OECD Publishing, Paris.

OECD (2012), *OECD Economic Surveys: Australia 2012*, OECD Publishing, Paris.

OECD (2013), *Commercialising Public Research: New Trends and Strategies*, OECD Publishing, Paris.

OECD (2014), *OECD Science, Technology and Industry Outlook 2014*, OECD Publishing, Paris.

OECD (2015a), *The Innovation Imperative: Contributing to Productivity, Growth, and Well-Being*, OECD Publishing, Paris.

OECD (2015b), *The Future of Productivity*, OECD Publishing, Paris.

OECD (2015c), "Compendium of R&D Tax Incentive Schemes: OECD Countries and Selected Economies, 2015", Measuring Tax Incentives, *www.oecd.org/sti/rd-tax-stats.htm*.

OECD (2015d), *Frascati Manual 2015: Guidelines for Collecting and Reporting Data on Research and Experimental Development*, OECD Publishing, Paris.

OECD (2015e), *OECD Economic Surveys: Ireland 2015*, OECD Publishing, Paris.

OECD (2016), "Enhancing the Contributions of Higher Educaction and Research Institutions to Innovation", Background Document, OECD High Level Event on the Knowledge Triangle, Paris, September 2016.

OFHIM (Office of Harmonisation in the Internal Market) (2013), "Intellectual Property Rights Intensive Industries: Contribution to Economic Performance and Employment in the European Union", *Industry-Level Analysis Report*, September.

Ontario Ministry of Finance (2014), "Ontario Business Research Institute Tax Credit", May.

Parliament of Australia (2016), "Industry Research and Development Amendment (Innovation and Science Australia) Bill 2016", Explanatory Memorandum, The Parliament of the Commonwealth of Australia, House of Representatives.

PC (Productivity Commission) (2007), *Public Support for Science and Innovation*, Research Report, Productivity Commission, Canberra.

PC (2016), *Intellectual Property Arrangements*, Draft Report, Canberra.

Penfield, T. et al. (2014), "Assessment, Evaluations, and Definitions of Research Impact: A Review", *Research Evaluation*, 23 (1), pp. 21-32.

PwC (PricewaterhouseCoopers) et al. (2015), *Innovate and Prosper: Ensuring Australia's Future Competitiveness Through University-Industry Collaboration*, PricewaterhouseCoopers, Australian Industry Group, Australian Technology Network of Universities.

State Government of Victoria (2016), *The CO2CRC Otway Project: Carbon Capture and Storage*, *www.energyandresources.vic.gov.au/energy/carbon-capture-and-storage/co2crc-otway-project*.

The Senate (2015), *Australia's Innovation System*, Economic References Committee, December.

The University of Sydney (2015), "Submission to Review of Research Policy and Funding Arrangements for Higher Education", September.

Universities Australia (2016a), "Universities Australia Submission to the Inquiry to the Australia's Future in Research Innovation", February.

Universities Australia (2016b), "Submission to R&D Tax Incentive Review", February.

Watt, I. (2015a), "Review of Research Policy and Funding Arrangements for Higher Education", Issues Paper, August.

Watt, I. (2015b), *Review of the Research Policy and Funding Arrangements*, Report, November.

Westmore, B. (2013), "R&D, Patenting and Productivity: The Role of Public Policy", *OECD Economics Department Working Paper*, No. 1046.

Williams, R. (2016), "Evaluating the Contribution of Higher Education to Australia's Research Performance", *The Australian Economic Review*, Vol. 49, No. 2, pp. 174-83.

ORGANISATION FOR ECONOMIC CO-OPERATION AND DEVELOPMENT

The OECD is a unique forum where governments work together to address the economic, social and environmental challenges of globalisation. The OECD is also at the forefront of efforts to understand and to help governments respond to new developments and concerns, such as corporate governance, the information economy and the challenges of an ageing population. The Organisation provides a setting where governments can compare policy experiences, seek answers to common problems, identify good practice and work to co-ordinate domestic and international policies.

The OECD member countries are: Australia, Austria, Belgium, Canada, Chile, the Czech Republic, Denmark, Estonia, Finland, France, Germany, Greece, Hungary, Iceland, Ireland, Israel, Italy, Japan, Korea, Latvia, Luxembourg, Mexico, the Netherlands, New Zealand, Norway, Poland, Portugal, the Slovak Republic, Slovenia, Spain, Sweden, Switzerland, Turkey, the United Kingdom and the United States. The European Union takes part in the work of the OECD.

OECD Publishing disseminates widely the results of the Organisation's statistics gathering and research on economic, social and environmental issues, as well as the conventions, guidelines and standards agreed by its members.

OECD PUBLISHING, 2, rue André-Pascal, 75775 PARIS CEDEX 16
(10 2017 06 1 P) ISBN 978-92-64-27149-4 – 2017